VEGETABLES
ARTICHOKES TO ZUCCHINI

Joe Famularo
Louise Imperiale

BARRON'S

ACKNOWLEDGMENTS

Thanks to our kitchen aides: Bernie Kinzer, Steve Leskody, John and Susan Imperiale; and special thanks to our overall expediter, Karen Lippert.

Photographic Credits
color photographs by Matthew Klein
food styling by Andrea Swenson
photo styling by Linda Cheverton

We are grateful to the following for supplying props for the photos: Cerelene, 55 East 57 Street, New York City, for Limoges Porcelain; Buccellati, 46 East 57 Street, New York City, for sterling silver flatware and serving pieces; Very Special Flowers, 215 West 10 Street, New York City, for flowers; Francoise Nunalle, 105 West 55 Street, New York City, for antique linen napkins.

Book design by Milton Glaser, Inc.

All inquiries should be addressed to:
Barron's Educational Series, Inc.
250 Wireless Boulevard
Hauppauge, New York 11788

International Standard Book No. 0-8120-1756-0

Library of Congress Catalog No. 93-21986

Library of Congress Cataloging-in-Publication Data

Famularo, Joe J.
    Vegetables: artichokes to zucchini / Joe Famularo, Louise Imperiale.
      p.   cm.
    Includes index.
    ISBN 0-8120-1756-0
    1. Cookery (Vegetables)   I. Imperiale, Louise.
II. Title.
TX801.F23   1993   93-21986
641.6'5—dc20   CIP

PRINTED IN HONG KONG

3456   880   987654321

CONTENTS

INTRODUCTION

If we had to choose one family of food to live with for the rest of our lives, we would choose vegetables. The variety is infinite: there are so many vegetables and so many ways to cook them. Moreover, we can't think of more beautiful things to look at. What can compare with the shape, color, or gleam of a bright red tomato? a smooth-as-silk, deep purple eggplant? the pure white cap of a mushroom? a bunch of carrots, with their fern-like ends? lacy celery hearts? fresh, pale green dandelion leaves? a majestic artichoke? a family of garlic cloves? the regal leek? the beauty and mystery of the inner rings of an onion?

This is not a book about vegetarian cooking; it is a book about vegetables. Our aim is not to put you on a vegetarian diet, but to encourage you to eat more vegetables and to prepare them with greater interest and inventiveness.

The choice of vegetables as our favorite food type is also based on the fact that they contain all the essentials of good nutrition: proteins, carbohydrates, fats (though only a little!), minerals, and vitamins. These elements vary in amount from one vegetable to the next, but in no other food group is there more complete nourishment. Without question, vegetables are essential to everyone's diet because most are rich in minerals and vitamins and almost all provide needed fiber, and all three nutrients are vital to health. Vitamin C is needed for the bones and teeth; Vitamin A for eyesight and healthy skin; iron, one of the many minerals in vegetables, is particularly essential for women during the childbearing years; and potassium guards against excess salt in the diet. Most vegetables are low in calories, and this is surely one of their best features.

All vegetables combine with meat, fish, poultry, game, pastas, and eggs. More importantly, they combine wonderfully with each other; think of a cool green salad composed of various lettuces, each with its own color, texture, and taste. The combination may be elaborated by adding basil or tarragon, parsley or peppers. Or try new beet leaves, sorrel, or the palest blush of a nasturtium bud.

Just thinking about vegetables can put anyone on a gastronomic spree. Imagine . . . .

Shredding zucchini and cooking it in sour cream, dill and paprika.

Combining boiled potatoes with lemon juice, butter, sugar, salt, freshly ground pepper, and finely chopped lemon zest.

🍏 Whipping up a casserole of zucchini, string beans, potatoes, and whole eggs. (Just break the eggs open over the vegetables in the baking pan, season with Parmesan cheese, garlic, basil, parsley, salt, and freshly ground pepper, and sprinkle fresh breadcrumbs overall.)

🍏 Heating chickpeas, sliced scallions, and slivers of roasted red pepper in an oil and vinegar dressing.

🍏 Stir-frying snow peas in peanut oil with a little salt, sugar, and several tablespoons of chicken stock.

🍏 Rolling thin slices of eggplant with ricotta, basil, and shallots, then baking them in a sauce of tomato and roasted pepper.

Slowly but surely, American eating habits are changing. Americans are eating considerably less meat than they did 10 years ago, and there is a national interest in good and better food, good health and preventive medicine. People today are obsessed with wholesome diets that are low in fat, high in fiber. Those who concentrate on eating more fresh vegetables, fruits, and whole grains, and who lower their intake of caffeine, sugar and salt, can have high expectations about improving their well-being and decreasing the chance of diet-related illnesses, which include high blood pressure, heart disease and cancer. We don't believe that you have to go to a health food store to eat properly, and nutritional experts agree on one important point: you can rarely go wrong with *fresh* food.

An important nutritional study was released in 1982 by the National Cancer Institute and the National Academy of Sciences Committee on Diet. The study's general conclusion was that good nutrition can reduce the risk of developing the three commonest cancer types in the United States: those of the breast, lung and colon. Briefly, the scientists and researchers recommended eating 1. high-fiber foods, 2. vegetables and fruits rich in Vitamin A, and 3. vegetables and fruits high in Vitamin C (especially vegetables in the cabbage family: broccoli, Brussels sprouts, cauliflower, collards, kale, kohlrabi, turnips, and watercress, for example. They also suggested reducing fat intake, as fat supplies many calories and few nutrients. (This does *not*, however, apply to infants under one year of age.)

For too many years, too many people have overcooked, underpresented, and deemphasized vegetables. Years have been spent developing new ways to cook meats and to elaborate on desserts. But the vegetable, or more often two of them — one usually a disgusting mush of tasteless mashed potatoes — was put on a dinner plate because it seems to belong there. Who doesn't recall the pile of overcooked green beans or carrots, devoid of a speck of seasoning?

Vegetables have been helped greatly by the interest in *nouvelle cuisine* and by the food revolution in general. Many now realize the importance of cooking *in* the nutrients, not cooking them out. The emphasis is on bright, natural colors in vegetables — they are there to begin with, so why destroy them? More books on vegetable cookery are appearing and that's a good sign. Most of these books, however, still suggest vegetables as a side dish. We feel strongly that this should change. Vegetables should take a more prominent position in the menu, as entree or main dish. Not all these preparations need avoid meat altogether — in fact, we like meat in some casseroles, loaves and vegetable rolls — but we believe it should be played down to accord with principles of good modern nutrition. There should be more dishes in which vegetables are combined for better taste, improved nutrition and abundant color. Terrines and tarts, salads and soups lend themselves to this treatment.

There should be a serious return of the vegetable plate, which presents three or four vegetables — interestingly flavored and arranged — as the main dish of the meal. The same goes for salads, in which lots of progress has been made. Adding to that progress is what this book is all about.

This is a book of opportunity — opportunity to improve your health through the vegetable kingdom. It is time to push vegetables to the center of your plate.

1

SOME BASICS ABOUT VEGETABLES

Refreshing and light, vegetables act well in any cooking method — baked or broiled, steamed or boiled, sautéed, or deep fried. One of the delights our world offers couldn't be simpler: fresh spring asparagus briefly boiled or steamed to the point of tenderness and touched by a hollandaise or vinaigrette sauce. Vegetables, crisply fried, offer incredible taste sensations: tender and succulent vegetable bites with contrasting crisp coatings.

STEAMING Steaming fresh vegetables over boiling water is an excellent way to preserve fresh flavor and nutrients. Almost any vegetable can be cooked in this way except, perhaps, for beets (it would take too long). Most vegetables can be steamed in less than 10 minutes; this, of course, will depend on the size and density of the vegetable. Julienned carrots, for example, will take considerably less time than whole or halved ones. Bamboo steaming containers with covers are available in Oriental markets and are not costly. To hold the water we have a skillet of the same diameter as the bamboo container, and it is a joy to use. It seems to last forever and is effortless to maintain.

BOILING Boiling vegetables is slightly faster than steaming them, but generally this method doesn't preserve as many nutrients. It is the preferred method for whole potatoes, beets, artichokes and other large, whole, dense vegetables. When boiling vegetables, use lots of water (the general rule is four quarts of water to one pound of vegetables) and add a little salt. If the vegetable contains tannin and will therefore discolor (artichoke is an example of this), add some fresh lemon juice; the juice of one lemon is adequate for four quarts boiling water. When boiling greens such as spinach or collards, leave the cover off to retain their color.

BAKING One of the simplest ways to cook vegetables is to bake them whole in their skins. Squashes, eggplants, tomatoes, and all root vegetables, most notably potatoes, are prime examples of this, because their skins protect the inner vegetable from drying out. We're all for baking whole onions, potatoes, sweet potatoes, and beets (beets are truly delicious when baked whole, by the way), but we think one of the best techniques with vegetables is combining them with each other and with other foods and baking them to enhance their flavors. Baked casseroles or vegetable stews are typical, and tremendously appetizing. A few things to keep in mind: (1) tightly pack vegetables in baking dishes to keep in moisture; (2) a few drops of olive or vegetable oil will enhance flavor and help prevent blistering and scorching; (3) cover baking containers tightly to keep in steam; (4) remember that many vegetables will render lots of juices as they cook (for example it usually isn't necessary to add water to a zucchini casserole); (5) baked vegetables are always good served hot, but many, for example ratatouille, are just as good cold; (6) some baked dishes will look better if they are run under the broiler for a minute or so.

BROILING   Other than for kebabs, broiling most vegetables is not especially common or advisable. Yet there are exceptions — we often broil eggplant slices and mushrooms, after coating them with olive or vegetable oil. The most important rule is not to leave the broiler even for a minute. Broiling heat is extremely intense, about 550°F, so it is important to brush vegetables frequently with butter, oil, or a marinade.

GRILLING   The concerns in grilling vegetables are similar to those in broiling; the heat is intense and, in fact, more uncontrollable than in broiling. But grilled vegetables are delicious. Cut slices — of eggplant, for example — thicker than for broiling, coat with oil, and baste as necessary. Corn, potatoes, onions, and tomatoes can be grilled successfully if they are wrapped. Aluminum foil is one of the best wraps to use, but also take advantage of the natural cornhusk as protector. Corn tied in its husk should be soaked in cool water for about 15 minutes and drained before grilling. When grilling potatoes, we remove a thin strip of skin, rub each potato with butter, oil or bacon grease, add salt and pepper, wrap in foil and then grill.

SOME THOUGHTS ABOUT PLANNING A MENU

One of the great pleasures in cooking with vegetables is the opportunity it gives you to be innovative and creative in planning a meal. We have concentrated on vegetables as main dishes in this book, but there is every opportunity for you to use some of the recipes as first courses or appetizers, with another as entree and still another as a side dish. Two examples of this are:

MENU 1

Appetizer: Artichokes Stuffed with Lamb *p. 108*
Entree: Gazpacho Terrine *p. 74*
Side Dish: Green Lettuce Salad *(Recipe not included in book.)*

MENU 2

Appetizer: Vegetable Cream Soup *p. 230*
Entree: Crepes Filled with
Spinach and Cheese Soufflé *p. 131*
Side Dish: Sliced Fresh Tomatoes *(Recipe not included in book.)*

It should be remembered that some vegetable main dishes do not provide all the protein we require. This is easy to deal with, however. Add grated cheese to soups, stews and casseroles, or garnish with slices of egg. Better yet, balance your menu by serving a protein-rich first course such as Lentil Salad, p. 209. Rice is a good source of protein, so have it with Vegetable Curry, p. 144, for example. Alternatively, add a protein-rich vegetable like beans or a spoonful of cottage cheese or ricotta. Another thought is to get your protein at dessert time. If you eat a hearty vegetable supper, a scoop of ice cream will add protein and sheer delight. Or what about fruit and nuts?

In any case, planning menus with recipes in this book should be not only simple, but fun. Here are three more ideas:

MENU 3

Appetizer: Corn and Lettuce Soup *p. 227*

Entree: Ratatouille Terrine Baked in Green Leaves *p. 76*

Side Dish: Parmesan Potatoes in a Charlotte Mold *p. 48*

MENU 4

Appetizer: Tomato Basil Soufflé *p. 191*

Entree: Spinach and Veal Loaf *p. 78*

Side Dish: White Potatoes Baked in Cream *p. 163*

MENU 5

Vegetable Curry with Ten Condiments, including Peach and Almond Chutney *p. 144*

WHAT VEGETABLES HAVE TO OFFER

Vegetables offer vitamins and minerals, and are a reliable source of carbohydrates. They also offer fiber, which is necessary for good health, and starch for food energy. Most dark green vegetables offer Vitamin C, iron, and B vitamins. The deep yellow vegetables and carrots offer Vitamin A; potatoes and tomatoes are also good sources of Vitamin C.

The U.S. Department of Agriculture has established grade standards for most fresh vegetables, and these standards are used mostly by growers, shippers, wholesalers, and retailers. If you see "U.S. No. 1" (almost always on carrots, potatoes, and onions), you can be fairly assured that these vegetables are fresh, tender, have good color, and are mainly free from decay. But remember this: the quality of most fresh vegetables can be judged easily by their external appearance.

Opposite: Cold Primavera Vegetable Mold (page 38).

2

VEGETABLES: ARTICHOKES TO ZUCCHINI

This alphabetical list has been prepared as a handy reference to help you buy, clean, and prepare vegetables. There are no set rules for buying vegetables; each has individual characteristics and values.

GLOBE ARTICHOKE, ITALIAN OR FRENCH

When artichokes are exposed to air the process of discoloration sets in, and an artichoke discolored to the point of blackness is a disagreeable sight. Select bright green ones with firm stems and don't assume that largeness is an indication of tenderness, for "good things come in small packages" where artichokes are concerned. One excellent way of testing for freshness is to cut off a piece of the stem; if the cut is white and somewhat juicy, the artichoke is young and fresh. Store artichokes in a plastic bag in the refrigerator, but only for a short time.

Enameled ironware works best for cooking artichokes, particularly if the vessel has a cover, but a stainless steel pan is fine, too. Carbon knives spell disaster in preparing artichokes because they will discolor the vegetable; use stainless steel knives.

The usual ways to prepare artichokes for cooking are to keep them whole, quarter them, or just use the artichoke hearts. To cook them whole, remove and discard the tough outer leaves, especially if they are discolored. Cut off the stem so that it is flush with the bottom of the artichoke. Make this a straight cut so that the vegetable stands easily. Lay the artichoke on its side and trim off the top third with one decisive cut. Snip off the prickly tops of the remaining leaves with scissors. To cook the artichokes in quarters, follow all steps for cooking them whole and then quarter them. Use a sharp knife to remove the furry choke just above the heart. To prepare artichoke hearts, remove the stem flush with the bottom and then cut away all the green leaf parts. Do not remove the choke at this point; it's easier to do that after the heart is cooked.

When you clean and prepare artichokes be sure to have handy a bowl of cool water to which you've added one or two tablespoons lemon juice. You will have to dip the artichokes into this mixture to prevent discoloration as you go along.

After they are pared (or "turned") and trimmed, it is very important to rub them with lemon juice and cover them with salted water.

JERUSALEM (SUNFLOWER)ARTICHOKE

This is not an artichoke and it doesn't come from Jerusalem. Belonging to the sunflower family and originally from the Mississippi and Missouri Valleys, the Jerusalem artichoke is a tuberous root that is naturally sweet, crunchy, and crispy, resembling the water chestnut.

Jerusalem artichokes almost always come in one-pound plastic bags. Feel them; they should be firm. They will keep for weeks in the vegetable compartment of the refrigerator. It is not necessary to peel them; instead, wash the tubers well and scrub with a stiff kitchen brush. The skin is delicate and most of it will brush away.

ARUGULA   This peppery-flavored leaf is a mysterious and most welcome addition to a salad. Called by many other names (roquette, ruchetta, rugula, rocket and rocket cress), it can be grown easily in spring as are other lettuces. If you grow arugula pick it young, as it will toughen and get too peppery as it matures. If you buy it, look for fresh leaves, not too large, and wash them several times in cool water. Spin dry or dry with toweling before adding to salads.

ASPARAGUS   The best-known asparagus varieties are white (the French Argenteuil, German, and Belgian types); the purple Italian or Genoa, and the commonly found green.

If you grow your own asparagus you know what it is like at its best, but most people have to depend on the local supermarket. Buy asparagus loose if you can, so that you can look it over carefully. Avoid plastic-wrapped bunches. The lower portion of the stem should be whitish with pink overtones, and the stem should be fairly smooth. Pick up a stalk: it should be firm, not limp.

To prepare for cooking, hold the stalk horizontally with both hands; bend it by moving your hands up or down to the point where it snaps or breaks in two. Discard the lower part of the stalk.

Use a vegetable peeler to peel the lower part of the usable stalk just as you would peel a potato, carrot or cucumber.

Asparagus are often filled with sand and grit. Soak them in cool, salted water for 30 minutes or longer, then rinse them several times before cooking. Stand the bunch upright in a narrow, deep vessel, and add boiling water up to the beginning of the flower portion (the tips cook by steaming.) We use a six- or eight-cup coffee percolator, which is an ideal cooking utensil for asparagus. The percolating cup unit is removed, of course, and the cover is put on. The cooking process rarely takes more than 10 minutes, less if the asparagus are really fresh.

A two-pound bunch of fresh asparagus can be stretched to serve six people, but it's better for four.

AVOCADO Like so many fruits, the avocado has a magnificent design: pear-shaped, its smooth flesh a beautiful pale green, and with one very large seed at its center. One of gastronomy's prime joys is slicing an avocado in half and opening it.

One pound of avocado contains 58.6 grams of fat, which makes it a dieter's horror. Nevertheless, this American tropical fruit with its Mexican, West Indian, and Guatemalan varieties has many uses as a "vegetable."

The best way to buy a ready-to-eat avocado is to pick it up and feel it; the flesh should yield slightly to pressure. The skin of a ripe avocado will be a darker green than that of the unripe one. If the avocado has soft or black spots, pass it up.

BASIL   In the *Great Herbal,* published in 1526, it is written that "Basil taketh away melancholy and maketh merry and glad." However, basil is an herb that was largely unpopular in the United States until the last two decades, when the pizza and pesto crazes helped it become better known. In the south of France, it has always been the queen of the herb world.

Pistou in Provence and pesto in Piedmont depend on several cupfuls of basil. There are at least half a hundred varieties of basil, but sweet basil is best because of its fabulous affinity for garlic and tomatoes. If you haven't yet grown basil, you should. A flowerpot will do, but if you give it space in the garden with lots of sun and air, one plant will sprout enough leaves to last all summer. Grow a dozen plants. Basil grows easily and profusely. It looks good, smells beautiful, and freezes superbly. Pick, wash, and dry the leaves; fill a one-pint plastic container, and freeze.

BEANS   The history of man could be written by examining the use of the bean. The ancient Romans, for example, used beans in their elections, voting pro with a white bean and con with a black one. Broad or butter, soy or string, fava or French — beans grow all over the world, in endless varieties. Who has not eaten haricot, kidney, navy or pinto bean?

DRIED BEANS   This category includes black-eyed peas, chickpeas, and lentils, as well as cranberry, great northern, kidney, lima, navy, pink, and pinto beans. All are among the least expensive but most nutritious foods. When served with rice, beans provide complete protein. Cholesterol-free, one pound of dried beans yields up to eight cups after cooking.

FAVA BEANS   This is the broad bean, not too well known in the United States, but a favorite for centuries in many European and North African countries. Favas are available fresh and dried, and are sometimes used in place of chickpeas. The fresh ones come in a very green pod from which they have to be removed like fresh peas. Buy fresh favas with bright, almost glossy green shells. The beans inside should be small and tender and can be eaten raw; if very large and yellow in color, they are too mature.

GREEN BEANS The best test for freshness in green beans is snapping them: when bent they should snap readily, not flex. Look for fresh color and crispness. Despite the old name "string beans," today's green beans are stringless. Only the ends need to be snapped off (some people cut them off, but it's more fun snapping).

Cook pole and wax beans as you do green beans, by steaming or by simmering uncovered until crisp-tender in a little bit of plain or salted water.

BEAN SPROUTS Bean sprouts are available in cans, but use fresh ones whenever you can; the difference is astonishing. It is popular today to grow your own, which is easy to do since sprouts mature in three or four days. Look for fresh ones in the markets; they should be whitish in color, with no trace of brown. Often the green husks are still on the beans, and although they are not harmful if eaten they should be removed before using in a recipe. The usual variety for sprouting is mung beans.

BEANS, YARD-LONG These Chinese green beans are similar to *haricots verts* in flavor but not in texture. You can't miss them in the markets, because they come in one- to three-foot lengths and are usually tied in a bunch at one end. Look for smooth, firm beans, and don't overcook them. They can be used many ways, cut in varying lengths, eaten hot or cold.

BEET GREENS These are delicious cooked with small, sugar-sweet beets still attached. The tenderest beet roots are less than two inches in diameter. We rarely see edible beet greens in the markets; they are almost always too mature.

BOK CHOY Although it may be interchangeable with celery cabbage in cooking, this vegetable, "bok choy," looks different. The thick stems are pure white; its wide leaves are green. It comes in bunches like celery, which have "hearts" also like celery. Of course, the hearts are more tender, tasty and delicate than the outer stalks. Look for firm stalks, clear colors, and fresh leaves, and remember that "bok choy" doesn't keep as long in the refrigerator as celery cabbage does.

BROCCOLI Buy broccoli with tightly closed buds and dark emerald green stalks. Do not buy yellowish blooms, which are usually wilted, and try to avoid stems that are too thick. A member of the cabbage family, broccoli is a joy to grow, for the more you cut the greater the yield.

The tender, thick stems are tasty. Peel them with a swivel peeler, then cut them into one-inch diagonal pieces to help cook them faster. Bring lots of water to a rapid boil, add a sprinkle of salt and then the broccoli. Cook uncovered to preserve the bright green color. The more water the better, because a large quantity will return more quickly to the boil once the broccoli has been put in.

CHINESE BROCCOLI This is not too different from its American counterpart but is sharper in flavor. It is also leafier and somewhat longer, with very small flowers. Treat it as you do regular broccoli when buying, cooking, and storing.

BROCCOLI RABE Broccoli rabe is a bitter-flavored cousin of broccoli. The stalks are thin and long and the leaves resemble those of regular broccoli. But broccoli rabe does not have the large, tightly closed heads of broccoli; instead, it has tufts of flowerets here and there throughout the stalks.

It's difficult to describe the origin of this tasty green vegetable; some believe it derives from the turnip or mustard green, but we don't think so. Nonetheless, you should try preparing it. Combined with olive oil, garlic and red pepper it is simply superb.

To add to the confusion about its origin, it is marketed under the names of broccoli rape, broccoli raab, and rappini. When buying it, look for firm, thin stems. Unlike broccoli, look for yellowish flowerets, but they will be quite small and somewhat open. Broccoli rabe is almost always in Italian markets, and is now available in most city supermarkets as well.

To prepare broccoli rabe, wash it well and trim off the ends. Remove the strings on the larger stalks just as you would on a large celery stalk. Cut the larger broccoli rabe leaves in half and let them stand in cool water until you are ready to cook them.

Heat two or three cups of water in a large saucepan. Add one teaspoon salt and bring the water to a rapid boil. Add the broccoli rabe and cook until just tender; depending on the size and freshness of the stalks, this will take five to 10 minutes. Remove from the boiling water immediately and drain.

BRUSSELS SPROUTS If you grow these, you know they can be unsightly and ungainly as they sprout large, tough leaves. But there's something exciting about the way tens of miniature cabbages hug the massive center stalk.

Always select small, tight and firm Brussels sprouts; they should be dark green. Before cooking, remove outer bruised leaves, make a criss-cross knife cut in the stem end and put the sprouts in cold salted water for about one hour.

B URDOCK We see and pick lots of this vegetable in the fields north of New York. It is a wild plant which grows profusely in temperate zones across the United States; it can also be purchased in Oriental markets. When we were children we knew burdock as "red feet"; the root end is purplish red, with the stalk and leaves a pale avocado green. When properly prepared, burdock is delicious.

Pick or choose young stems about one foot long. To prepare, hold the stalk leaf end up in one hand. Pull down on the leaves to peel the stalk, leaving two or three small leaves at the top. Bend the stalk at a tender point as you would asparagus, and snap it; discard the root end. Wash usable stems in cool water several times and drain.

C ABBAGE A split in a cabbage is a sign of its excessive age; so is a strong cabbage odor. Young, tender cabbage does not smell strong and is usually tightly packed. Choose the younger head of cabbage, for it is tastier and more tender. Discard the outer leaves (there is less waste on a younger head because fewer outer leaves usually have to be removed), cut the head into quarters, and soak the pieces in cool salted water for 15 to 20 minutes.

C ELERY CABBAGE Known also as Peking cabbage, this is a tightly formed long vegetable with wide, white, pale green- or yellow-tipped leaves. Feel it for compactness and look for fresh leaves. It is usually sold by the pound and it will keep for days, unwashed, in the refrigerator.

C ARDOON A member of the thistle or artichoke family, cardoons are also called "chard" in the United States, and the leaf ribs are sometimes called "beet-chard." The stalks grow three to four feet tall and are full of flavor. The ribs can be used as asparagus, the leaves as spinach. Try serving cardoons with stews containing tomatoes, for they are delicious together.

CARROTS One of the foods richest in Vitamin A, fresh young carrots are bright orange with just a speck of green coloring at the stem end. If this end has too much green, the carrot is probably overgrown and more tough than tender. Most carrots come in plastic packages, but don't be afraid to peer through the plastic to check for green ends. And don't let it stop you from grasping the carrots to check for firmness.

Carrots are almost as versatile as potatoes. They can be peeled (or not), chopped, sliced, cubed, or cut in fancy shapes. They are served hot or cold, in soups, salads, cakes, and casseroles. They can be candied or creamed, molded or minted. For centuries, they have been combined with peas, onions, or celery; with cream, butter, or sugar.

When carrots are new and small, peeling is not necessary. Run them under cool water and use a small kitchen brush to clean them. Fresh carrots are available all year, so there is no need to use frozen ones. Avoid canned carrots if at all possible.

CAULIFLOWER When you buy cauliflower, select a white head with tightly packed flowers and fresh green leaves. If the flesh has discolored, the flowers have spread, or the leaves have grayed, you'll have a tough, chewy vegetable.

To prepare the whole head, remove the leaves and scoop out most of the stalk. This is done by turning the cauliflower upside down, carving with a paring knife into the center stalk, and removing the bulk of it. Don't cut too deeply, or you'll end up with flowerets instead of a whole cauliflower.

Put the head into salted cool water for at least 30 minutes; according to old family folklore, this is the way to rid the head of any worms. Cauliflower steams well; it will take less than 10 minutes for flowerets and up to half an hour for the full head.

CELERIAC This is also known as celery root, for it is grown for its root rather than its stalks (although the stalks are edible also). Celeriac has a strong, wonderful celery flavor and is famous prepared as the classic *céleri rémoulade*. But it is also used in many other ways these days. It is a round vegetable, white inside and brownish outside. When buying celeriac, avoid any larger than four inches (about the size of a man's fist). Store it in the refrigerator no longer than a week. Celeriac should be peeled before cooking.

CELERY One of the tastiest vegetables, with a myriad of uses — it is delicious just to eat it raw, and a celery heart is a real treat.

Celery is a satisfying vegetable to grow, but it is available, everywhere almost throughout the year. Look for fresh, un-packaged bunches with light green leaves, and feel the celery for crispness. Use the tender leaves in cooking; they add considerable flavor.

COLLARDS A member of the cabbage family and very popular in the southern part of the United States — but we find collards at our greengrocer's all the time, so they must be coming north. Our father said that anything in the cabbage family always tasted better after the frost hit it. We agree, and this is true for collards as well as for kale, savoy cabbage, brussels sprouts, and so on. Don't buy overly large or yellowish leaves. Collards do not have the bright, dark leaves that spinach does, but they should be reasonably crisp and green.

CORN Corn is now a staple all over the world, yet it may be even more American than the proverbial apple pie. It was first carried to Europe by Columbus, but within two generations of his voyage to the New World the vegetable was known throughout Europe and as far afield as Africa, India, China, and

Tibet. The corn plant is hardy as well as practical; every part of it is used for one purpose or another.

The ideal way to cook corn is fresh from the garden; husk it and cook it as quickly as you can. But for most of us, this is rarely possible. Fortunately, refrigerating the corn helps keep it fresh for a little while longer. To check for freshness there is our grandmother's fingernail test: press a fingernail into a kernel (even if you have to open the husk). If you discover milky drops, your chances that the ear of corn is young and tender are increased. Buy ears of corn with fresh-looking, green husks. Open the husk; the kernels should be plump, but not too large and moist-looking. The same is true for both yellow and white corn.

We think the best way to cook corn on the cob is to combine water and milk in equal amounts to cover the corn, then bring the liquid to a boil. Put the ears of corn into the boiling liquid, cover, and cook for 6 or 7 minutes. The best way to serve corn on the cob is with softened butter, salt, and pepper. Don't throw any leftover corn away. Cut off the kernels and freeze them.

CUCUMBERS Beware of oversized cucumbers, especially if they are very thick and have any yellowish or brownish parts. The color should be bright green, the size small, the fruit firm.

EGGPLANT Known for thousands of years as the *mala insana* (the "raging apple"), eggplant was always soaked in cold salt water to remove its insanity. Today it is common to salt and drain it, not for fear of its poisonous drippings, but because this makes it less bitter. The importance of the salting process is directly related to the size of the eggplant: the larger the vegetable, the more essential the salt.

Buy smaller-sized eggplants, and make sure the lovely green, capelike bracts and stem are firmly attached. If the bracts are loose it is likely that the vegetable has aged and started to spoil. The eggplant should also be firm. An eggplant that is beginning to shrivel is easy to recognize; don't buy it. Seeds should be snow white. Of course, there is no way to check the whiteness of the seeds in the shop, but you can check the stems and bracts.

The eggplant, *aubergine*, or *melanzana* is versatile. It can be cubed, sliced, julienned, halved; pureed, sautéed, creamed, baked, grilled. An international star, it is prepared *à la grecque*, *à la turque*, *à la portugaise*, *à la catalane*, and *à l'italienne*. And although eggplant can be cooked either peeled or unpeeled, it seems useless to remove its beautiful skin.

CHINESE OR JAPANESE EGGPLANT This looks like American eggplant but it has a long sculptured shape and its color is deeper. It can be prepared in the same way as American eggplant and the small Italian variety, and the rules for buying and storing the vegetable are the same as for the other types.

ENDIVE This vegetable is becoming more popular in American restaurants and homes, and deservedly so. Some endive is grown in the United States, but the quality of the Belgian variety is considered superior.

Endive is usually four to six inches long and one to two inches wide; its many leaves are white to pale yellow, fitted tightly together and tapering to a point. One pound of endive usually produces four individual pieces, enough for four servings. The calorie count per serving is under 20.

Europeans treat endive in as many ways as Americans treat potatoes. It is buttered, braised, and bechameled; souped, souffléed, and tossed in salads; pureed, Parmesaned, and sprinkled with pepper.

For example, *roulade au jambon* combines a cooked and chilled endive with a slice of ham and chopped aspic; most often it is served *au gratin*. An unusual dish is half an endive, raw, filled with a combination of steak tartare and Roquefort cheese.

FENNEL Fennel is used both as a flavoring and as a vegetable. Although it is only now gaining popularity in the United States, it has always been a favorite in Europe. This anise-flavored vegetable, sometimes called sweet or Roman fennel, grows profusely in Italy, France, Greece and other Mediterranean countries. Modern Italians make as much fuss over fennel as the ancient Romans did.

Fresh fennel is a large white bulb with pale green, feathery leaves. The bulb should be snow white and firm when you buy it. It is an excellent source of Vitamin A and very low in calories; dipped in olive oil and seasoned with salt and freshly ground pepper, is a good *crudité*.

GINGER A joyful root, deeply "rooted" in history, ginger was known in many ancient civilizations—Indian, South Asian, Chinese, Arabic, Roman, Greek. The tuber resembles an iris root. It has a paper-thin, light brown skin that can be peeled off with a parer. It freezes well, grates well, slivers well. Probably its most popular use is in gingerbread or cookies, but its essence is also found in ale, beer, and wine.

Ginger is one of the most exciting flavors, and its use is no longer limited to Chinese cooking. Most supermarkets now sell it as a staple. It will keep in the refrigerator for a week or so, but it's easier to freeze ginger (it keeps frozen for months) and use it as you need it. Frozen, it grates easily.

JICAMA A plain brown root vegetable. In California, they peel and slice jicama; it is sweet and crisp and gaining in availability. Best known as a *crudité*, it makes a good alternative to potato chips when served with dips.

KALE This green is more popular than some others, but usually it is cooked to death. Buy unpackaged leaves, and better still those on iced or refrigerated racks. Choose bright, crisp leaves; turn away from bruised ones, large leaves with excessive sand, and woody stems with thickly veined leaves. When storing kale, if you must, keep it in the coldest part of the refrigerator and do not wash the leaves first. Before cooking, wash it very carefully and remove the thicker stems.

KOHLRABI Popular in the Far East for centuries, this wonderful vegetable is making its appearance in many supermarkets across the country. Its flavor is most delicate and somewhat nutty, but it should not be peeled before cooking or the flavor will diminish.

Kohlrabi can be used in most of the ways one uses turnips and radishes. When cooked, it is delicious with sour cream and dill; served raw, it is excellent sliced thin with any good herb dip. Buy bulbs three inches or less in diameter, as these are the tender young ones. If you cook the leaves with the bulbs they will intensify the flavor.

LEEKS Leeks are an important member of the onion family, but as a rule the leek is sweeter and milder. The leek is probably as old as the fig, historically speaking. No one seems able to determine its origin, although it was grown in ancient Egypt and Rome. Its infinitely greater popularity in Europe than in the United States is difficult to understand, because it is easy to grow, almost totally free of diseases and pests, and unperturbed by frost. In Dutchess County, about 70 miles north of New York City, we leave leeks in the ground until Thanksgiving. They're easy to dig up, clean and freeze.

Don't buy leeks with discolored tops or any that are very large. They must be washed very carefully, because sand is often lodged between the layers (much of the leek grows underground). Cut off the root end and slice the leek down the middle. This makes it easy to separate and wash.

LETTUCE Lettuce comes in all shapes (and some colors, such as red leaf) and is available always. Bibb is more expensive, but it is often worth the difference in price because it tastes marvelous and has almost no waste. Boston lettuce is excellent and makes a delicious salad, as does romaine or Cos lettuce which grows in tight, upright heads. In any mention of lettuce we have to add two varieties of chicory—not really lettuces, but excellent salad greens—escarole and endive.

Again, look for vegetables that are not packaged and that are tightly formed (the only way to test for this is to pick up the head of lettuce and feel it). If it looks or feels mushy, leave it.

LOTUS ROOT This vegetable, so basic to Asian cooking, is now found in every Chinese market in the U.S. and in many supermarkets and specialty greengrocers. The root is sweet and starchy, while its leaves are flavorful and fragrant and often used as a food wrapper. The root is sausage-shaped and bulbous. Though peeled before cooking, it will turn dark if exposed to air so put it in water as soon as it's peeled or use it quickly.

Look for a firm bulb and fresh leaves when buying lotus root. It is probably wise to purchase it from a Chinese or other Asian greengrocer.

SILK MELON Also called silk squash, pleated squash, and Chinese okra, this is a dark green, ridged vegetable, one to two feet long and as many inches in diameter. The flesh is sweet and spongy; the skin is coarse.

The ridges are usually removed when preparing this vegetable for cooking, but the green skin between the ridges is left on. Be careful not to overcook it.

Look for firm, unscarred melons; avoid oversized ones and any with soft spots. Buy in Asian markets or specialty green-grocers.

MUSHROOMS Select mushrooms that are firm, clean, and unblemished; there should be no gray spots. It is better to buy them loose than prepackaged, even though they may cost a little more that way. Our experience with buying prepackaged mushrooms has not always been satisfactory: as is the case with packaged strawberries, the top layer is often for show, with lower layers degenerating in quality. Besides, it's fun to reach into the bins and handpick each mushroom.

Don't peel mushrooms. Wipe or lightly brush them with a dampened tea towel or paper towel. Trim the stem ends and reserve them, usually in the freezer, for soups and stocks.

OKRA Buy these small, no longer than two or three inches. (If you grow okra, pick them before they get to this size.) They are available in the markets frozen, canned or bottled more often than fresh, and these may be used successfully. Okra is more often used for its thickening properties, as for gumbo, than as a flavoring agent.

ONIONS Onions are easy to grow (especially from "sets") and easy to store, but yellow, white and purple onions are everywhere. They are also canned whole and frozen in minced form.

It's difficult to think of any cuisine without this wonderful vegetable, and it is rare to find a bad onion in the shops — probably because turnover is so rapid. It is probably best to buy two or three pounds at a time; ours sit in a bowl on the kitchen table, and I don't think we've hit a rotten one yet. It's a good idea, however, to feel the onions for firmness when you buy; also, they shouldn't be sprouting.

Opposite: Sweet Red Pepper Strips with
Enoki Mushrooms (page 216).

PARSNIPS There are several kinds of parsnip, the round or turnip parsnip and the long carrot-shaped varieties being the more popular and easily available. They have been around for a long time, and are mostly used in stews and soups. We think there really isn't too much to be done with them; why puree parsnips when so many other vegetables puree to a better taste? When buying them, look for firm ones with few scars. They keep for days in a vegetable crisper, refrigerated.

PEAS Nonna, our grandmother, had an easy and wonderful market test for fresh peas which we called the "fingernail pea-pod press." She would hold a pea pod in her hand and press a cut into the pod with the fingernail of her thumb or index finger. If she didn't buy a pound or two of peas, it was because no moisture had appeared in the cut. But if the cut was moist, the peas were fresh and the sale was consummated. Nonna would also simply pick up a pea pod, open it, and eat the peas to test for freshness. Because we frequently accompanied her on her shopping jaunts, we were often recipients of a pea or two, but it was Nonna who made the decision to buy or pass.

When buying pea pods, look for those that are shiny and free of wrinkles. Fresh pea pods have a bright and beautiful green color. One pound of unshelled peas is not a large quantity when it comes to the finished product. For six people buy two or three pounds of unshelled peas.

Peas should be steamed or cooked in very little water. If you have very young fresh peas, cook them without water: melt 1 tablespoon butter in a small pan, add 1 pound shelled peas, and cover them with several lettuce leaves (washed but not dried). Cover the pan and cook slowly until the peas are tender. Add salt, pepper, and more butter if you wish. Fresh peas are the ultimate, but frozen peas do well. There is no reason at all to use canned peas.

SNOW PEAS A truly wonderful vegetable if fresh; frozen snow peas simply miss out on all the qualities of their fresh cousins. Snow peas are similar to fresh green peas, but much more delicate. The pod is the main attraction — crisp, tender and bright green. Look for good color, crisp and small pods.

Snow peas keep in the refrigerator for about two weeks. They almost always take less than a minute to cook. Remove the ends as for string beans, and some of the larger snow peas will need to have strings removed. These usually pull off when you remove the ends.

CHILI PEPPERS Fresh green chili peppers are very hot and should be used with caution. They tend to be more fiery than the red ones, because these peppers sweeten as they ripen. Don't touch your eyes or lips when seeding or cutting them; in fact, it is suggested that you wear rubber gloves while handling chilis. Look for crisp, unwrinkled peppers; they should be small and taut. They last in plastic bags in the refrigerator for a week or longer.

SWEET AND HOT PEPPERS Bell peppers, which are very full and round, may be green, yellow, red or purplish-black. They have many uses and can be prepared in many ways; one of the most popular treatments is to stuff them. Feel them for firmness before buying them, and be sure they still have stems. If they are overripe or have soft spots and are beginning to wrinkle, avoid them. Sweet Hungarian or banana peppers are longer, tapered, and usually a golden yellow; they are delicious. In addition to ordinary hot red peppers, there are also the cherry and cayenne peppers — both very hot and usually used in seasoning meats, sausages, vegetables and pasta.

RADISHES There are four main types of radishes: red, white icicle, black and daikon (Japanese or Oriental). In spite of the color on the outside, they are all white inside. Their skins, especially the black ones, are sharp and piquant. Radishes, available all year, are inexpensive and low in calories. If you eat enough of them, they provide a good Vitamin C supplement to your diet.

When buying red radishes look for bright coloring. Buy fresh bunches with the leaves on, not radishes packed in plastic bags. Smaller size radishes have more flavor, especially when eaten whole and raw. Store with the tops on in plastic bags in the refrigerator and soak in ice water for a half hour or longer to freshen and crisp.

The white radish is narrow and almost six inches long. It should be scraped with a vegetable peeler before serving. Store as for red radishes, immersing in ice water before serving.

Black radishes look like black turnips and should be firm and dark in color. Don't wash before storing, and before using be sure to peel with a vegetable peeler.

Daikon can be huge, but don't buy the overgrown ones — it's been reported that some weigh 50 pounds. Buy firm ones no larger than two to two and a half inches in diameter and eight to ten inches long. The skin must be peeled before using.

All these radishes have a longer refrigerator life (one to three weeks) than many other vegetables. Americans use radishes mostly for decoration; here's a chance to break away.

SALSIFY   A long, delicately flavored root, resembling the oyster in flavor. It comes in two varieties: white and black. An easy way to cook salsify is to peel the roots well and boil them in salted water for 45 minutes or longer, until tender. Then drain the salsify and rub or brush off the skin. If you don't use the roots right away, be sure to put them in water with some lemon juice to keep them from discoloring.

Salsify is excellent in soup and its leaves, if fresh, can be used as a cooked green or in salads. When buying, look, of course, for fresh leaves and firm roots.

SORREL   Sorrel's acidity is refreshing and can sharpen the taste of other vegetables when combined with them (and it can do the same for fish, meat and eggs). It is, happily, gaining in popularity in this country. Look for fresh, crisp greens and avoid limp or yellow-looking leaves. Store in plastic containers in the refrigerator; sorrel may be frozen in the same way.

YELLOW CROOKNECK SQUASH   This is a gourd with seeds inside and a buttery yellow rind. It is a summer variety, picked before it matures, and is tender enough to eat rind and all. Very popular, yellow squash is available in almost every market. When buying, choose small squash about four to six inches long. Although the rind may seem a bit heavy, it will pierce easily if it is fresh. The squash will keep for almost a week in plastic bags or containers. It cooks quickly and easily.

SWISS CHARD   Spinach is a beautiful green vegetable and is used in many ways, but Swiss chard is great, too. It's also easy to grow.

Chard looks like oversized spinach with very long white stems. Use it in place of spinach. When buying Swiss chard, go for a deep green color with crinkly and crisp leaves. Discard the large, overgrown leaves and use the smaller ones. As for the stems, peel them, as if stringing celery stalks; cut them into one- or two-inch lengths, and cook them with the greenery.

TURNIPS AND RUTABAGAS   The popular turnip has a beautiful lavender top, but the interior flesh is white. Often it is sold with its leaves. With or without tops, turnips are usually available all year long. Buy the small to medium size that are round, firm and smooth. If you see them in bunches with the tops on, be sure the tops are fresh and have a good green color.

Rutabagas are related to turnips but have yellow flesh and are much larger than turnips. They are usually sold with a waxy coating of paraffin, which helps keep in moisture and prevents shriveling and shrinkage. The coating is easy to remove before cooking; simply peel or cut it off. Don't buy bruised, oddly shaped or soft rutabagas. Get those that are smooth, round and heavy in weight.

Zucchini Zucchini has become a staple in most households, summer and winter, and zucchini bread — all-American in origin — is almost as popular as apple pie. *Courgettes*, Italian marrows, Italian squash, *zuchette*, *courge*, or *coccozelle* — call it what you will, zucchini is a favorite vegetable.

As versatile as the potato, the zucchini is a special vegetable because it combines beautifully with so many other foods. For example, prepared *à l'indienne*, zucchini simmer in butter with salt and curry and are covered with *una salsa besciamella*. *Courgettes à la niçoise* calls for flouring the zucchini and sautéing them in oil, then combining them with tomatoes and onions that have also been cooked in oil.

If you layer them in a gratin dish, combine them with rice cooked in stock and tomatoes, and add onions, garlic, and parsley, you will have courgettes *à la Provençale*. Originally in the south of France, and now in many other parts of the world, zucchini is also prepared with a stuffing of risotto flavored with Parmesan, garlic, and tomato puree, topped with breadcrumbs, and sprinkled with oil and chopped parsley. The Creoles are known to turn zucchini into jam by browning them in fat, salting them, and allowing most of the cooking liquid to evaporate until the mixture turns to an amber color, stirring and cooking all the while.

Buy young zucchini, small, firm, smooth, and with bright green skins. The best size is about one inch thick and six inches long, or smaller. Zucchini is perishable; keep it under refrigeration and use it within a week.

3

MOLDS, MOUSSES, AND ASPICS

Cooking is easier, and surely more enjoyable, these days because so many exciting ingredients are available. So much inspiration is gained just from looking around markets, smelling, seeing and touching the luscious vegetables and fruits, fragrant herbs and spices — all waiting to be tried. It's wonderful how once you start experimenting in the kitchen, one idea flows into another and the discoveries seem endless. It is especially true in this section, where a variety of vegetables combine to form healthy and nutritious food that is high in fiber, mostly low in sugar, and refreshingly inexpensive.

Aspic has many uses — as a garnish, mixed with mayonnaise to thicken it, or combined with vegetables, meat, poultry, or fish in savory molds. It is the transparent, pale amber-colored jelly that is prepared from stock flavored with herbs and vegetables.

The French word for foam or froth is *mousse,* the essence of which is lightness. As main dishes or on the buffet table mousses can be served hot or cold. Their shapes are varied and interesting, resulting from timbales, charlotte molds, ring molds, ceramic soufflé dishes, oval glass baking dishes — almost any type of container appealing to your taste will do. Mousses can incorporate both cooked and uncooked vegetables. They are enhanced by a variety of sauces, accompaniments and garnishes. Timbales and darioles become richer in taste and appearance when served atop smooth and delicate vegetable sauces or pale green, satiny mayonnaise.

Chef's Salad in Aspic

SERVES 8

Fresh vegetables and some meats make this a different chef's salad. It's very eye-appealing, with good flavor.

¼ cup cream Sherry
¼ cup cool water
2 packets (¼ ounce each) unflavored
  gelatin
3½ cups clarified Chicken Stock
8 slices bacon, cooked until crisp,
  drained
several sprigs of flat-leaf parsley
1 cup cooked turkey or chicken breast
  cut into ½-inch cubes
1 cup cooked ham cut into ½-inch cubes
1 cup Gruyère cheese cut into ½-inch
  cubes

¼ cup finely chopped fresh parsley
¼ cup finely chopped celery hearts with
  leaves
¼ cup finely chopped green onions

SOUR CREAM DRESSING
(makes 1 generous cup)
1 cup sour cream
2 tablespoons sugar
2 teaspoons Dijon mustard
1 tablespoon white wine vinegar
salt
freshly ground pepper

1 Combine Sherry, water, and gelatin and let stand until gelatin is softened, about 5 minutes. Heat chicken stock, add gelatin, and stir until completely dissolved. Oil a 2-quart mold (a nicely rounded ceramic or glass bowl will do well here) and pour in about 1 inch of the aspic; refrigerate until almost set. Refrigerate the remaining aspic until it begins to thicken.

2 When the molded aspic has begun to set, remove mold from refrigerator and weave bacon slices on it by laying 4 slices one way, 4 the other. Set flat parsley leaves in open spaces.

3 Add the turkey or chicken, ham and Gruyère cubes plus the chopped parsley, celery and onions to the slightly thickened aspic. Mix well; taste and adjust seasoning. Pour into mold. Refrigerate until completely set (about 3 hours) or overnight.

4 To make the dressing, combine all ingredients in a bowl and whisk until smooth. Unmold salad; serve with dressing.

Cold Primavera Vegetable Mold

SERVES 8

Filled with spring vegetables in a tangy mayonnaise sauce, this mold is beautiful and very tasty. It needs no additional saucing and is delicious served with dry, thin toast triangles or hot buttered cornbread. See photo 1 opposite page 12.

2 cups cooked broccoli flowerets (no larger than 1 inch)
1 cup cooked green beans, cut into 1-inch lengths
2 cups cubed cooked zucchini (about 3 thin ones, 1 × 6 inches, cut into ¼-inch cubes)
2 cups shredded cooked carrots (3 large; use large holes of hand grater, shredder, or processor)
½ cup finely chopped green onions
1 cup slivered snow peas (about 24, cut diagonally into ¼-inch slivers)
2 cups cubed fresh tomatoes (about 2 medium-large, in ½-inch cubes)
¼ cup finely chopped fresh parsley
juice of 1 lemon
2 tablespoons chili oil
1 cup toasted walnuts (toast walnuts in 350° oven with 1½ teaspoons butter until they begin to turn color)

1 cup ½-inch cubes of fontina cheese
¼ cup tarragon vinegar or white wine vinegar
1 tablespoon finely chopped fresh tarragon or 1 teaspoon dried
3 packets (¼ ounce each) unflavored gelatin
2 cups homemade Mayonnaise (page 261)
salt
freshly ground pepper
3 egg whites

TO ASSEMBLE
4 whole Kirby cucumbers, about 1½ × 5 inches
12 cooked ¼ × 3-inch carrot sticks
12 cooked ¼ × 3-inch green bean slivers
1 round carrot slice, about 1 inch in diameter and ¼ inch thick

1 Cook broccoli, beans, zucchini, and carrots separately in boiling salted water; do not overcook. Drain cooked vegetables and pat dry with paper or cotton toweling. Transfer to large mixing bowl. Add green onions, snow peas, tomatoes, parsley, lemon juice, and chili oil and toss lightly. Add walnuts and cheese and toss.

2 In a small saucepan, gently heat vinegar and tarragon with gelatin, stirring constantly, until gelatin is completely dissolved (this will be a very thick mixture and will only take a minute or two to dissolve over low heat). Cool to room temperature (placing pan in refrigerator will hasten cooling) and blend into mayonnaise. Add salt and pepper to taste and combine with vegetable mixture.

3 Whisk egg whites until they form soft peaks and fold into vegetable mixture. Taste for proper seasoning and adjust if necessary.

4 To assemble, wash and scrub cucumbers and cut off ends. Use a vegetable peeler to remove most of the skin, but leave some skin on. Slice cucumbers lengthwise into approximately 6 thin slices. Put in iced salted water until ready to use.

5 Prepare carrots and green beans as above; select straight beans, as they will be easier to place in mold. Add vegetables to cucumbers in iced water.

6 Put the carrot circle in the center bottom of a ceramic soufflé dish 3 inches deep and approximately 9 inches in diameter. Fit slices of cucumber on bottom, fanning out from circle like spokes of a wheel and leaving enough room between slices to fit in beans and carrots, alternately. Use scissors to shape and cut cucumber. Cut and fit cucumber slices up the sides, placing them in same position as bottom slices. Do the same with beans and carrots. This will create lines of cucumber, beans and carrots running from center of dish to outer bottom edge and up sides of dish.

7 When cooled and slightly thickened, pour vegetable/mayonnaise mixture carefully into vegetable-lined mold, pressing down with rubber spatula or back of spoon (you may have a little filling left over). Cover with plastic wrap and refrigerate for several hours or overnight, until mousse is set.

8 To unmold, immerse soufflé dish in hot water for a few seconds several times. Put an attractive serving plate or platter over mousse, invert and carefully shake soufflé dish to loosen mousse. Lift soufflé dish off and unmold mousse.

Hot Primavera Vegetable Mold

SERVES 8

One of the most spectacular vegetable preparations in this book, great for a buffet or dinner party.

32 asparagus spears
2 cups fresh broccoli flowerets
8 fresh snow peas, cut diagonally into
    ½-inch pieces (½ cup)
8 ounces fresh green peas, shelled, or
    5 ounces (½ package) frozen (about
    1 cup)
4 large boiling potatoes peeled, cut
    into ½-inch cubes and cooked until
    tender (about 3 cups loosely packed)
½ cup rich chicken stock or vegetable
    broth, cooked down to ¼ cup

½ cup whipping cream
2 garlic cloves, finely chopped
pinch of red pepper flakes
6 eggs
¾ cup freshly grated Parmesan cheese
2 tablespoons finely chopped fresh
    parsley
4 tablespoons (½ stick) butter
½ cup toasted pine nuts

1 Clean each vegetable by paring, washing, stringing, and slicing where necessary. Cook the asparagus, broccoli, peas and potatoes separately in boiling salted water until tender; do not overcook.

2 In a saucepan heat stock or broth, cream, garlic, and pepper flakes. Remove from heat as soon as mixture begins to boil.

3 In a large bowl combine eggs, cheese, and parsley and mix well. Add the cream mixture and stir well.

4 Heat ½ tablespoon butter in a small skillet and sauté the snow peas for 1 minute. Remove from heat and set aside. Preheat oven to 350°F.

5 Add 2 tablespoons butter to the potatoes and toss lightly. Add the cream and egg mixture, snow peas, and green peas to the potatoes, tossing lightly but well. Taste and adjust seasoning.

6 Liberally butter a mold 3½ inches deep and 8¼ inches wide at the top (a French soufflé dish is excellent). Cut out a circle of waxed paper to fit the bottom of the mold. Butter the top side of the paper. Arrange the broccoli flowerets on the bottom of the mold, flower sides down; there will be enough flowers to tightly cover the bottom of the dish. Arrange the asparagus stalks, after cutting to the length of the depth of the mold, standing up with the flower side of the asparagus pointed to the bottom of the mold.

7 Transfer the potato mixture to the mold. Place the mold in a large vessel filled with hot water and set both in the oven for 50 minutes, or until mold is firm; if it isn't, bake longer. Remove baking dish from the oven and from the water bath and let cool at least 30 minutes. Run a thin sharp knife around the outer edge of the mold to ease unmolding. Place a large serving plate over the mold, invert it, and allow it to sit for several minutes. Remove baking dish from the mold. There should be no juices in the dish; the mold should be set like a custard. Lift off the paper.

8 When it is turned out, sprinkle toasted pine nuts overall. Slice through mold as you would a cake. Serve with hot or cold tomato sauce, pages 257–259. The tomato sauce should be spooned onto each serving plate beside the serving, not directly over it.

NOTE

Asparagus spears are ideal in this preparation, but if for some reason you can't get good, fresh, firm ones, about ½ inch thick, other vegetables can be used: for example, a combination of green beans and carrots (cut into ½- × 3-inch strips), using 5 beans upright and then 3 carrot strips, and repeating all around the mold. Slices of zucchini (1 inch × 3 inches) interspersed with carrot strips will also work well. Arrange vegetables as close together as you can to prevent too much custard from showing.

Vegetables in Aspic with Cold Filet Mignon Slices

❦

SERVES 8

The combination of vegetables is glorious here, and you won't believe the beauty of this dish when it is turned out. Small filets of beef are grilled and sliced thinly, overlapped and set down the middle of the arrangement. The horseradish sauce is a must.

3 filet mignon steaks, each 5 or
   6 ounces (no larger)
2 garlic cloves, minced
1 tablespoon butter
salt
freshly ground pepper
10 pimiento-stuffed green olives,
   halved lengthwise
4 beets, cooked, cooled, and thinly sliced
12 to 20 asparagus spears, cooked and
   cooled

3 whole carrots, julienned, cooked,
   and cooled
24 shallots, peeled and cooked in
   water to cover with 2 tablespoons
   sugar, drained, and cooled
3 large mushrooms, thinly sliced
2 tablespoons chopped fresh parsley
2 quarts clarified beef stock
4 packets (¼ ounce each) unflavored
   gelatin

1 Prepare the filet mignon for broiling by first combining garlic and butter, mashing them to a paste and spreading it over filets on both sides. Salt and pepper each side. Broil filets until medium rare. When done, let stand until cool enough to handle, then cut into ¼-inch slices. Halve each slice crosswise. Cut away any fat or gristle. Set aside.

2 Prepare vegetables as above. Cool vegetables by running under cold water as soon as you remove from heat. Keep vegetables separate.

3 Put 2 cups stock in a bowl and add all the gelatin. Meanwhile, heat remaining 6 cups stock to simmering point, add gelatin mixture and stir over low heat until gelatin is completely dissolved. Remove from heat, cool and refrigerate until gel begins to thicken, but first ladle or spoon enough into a 9 × 14 × 2½-inch oval glass dish to cover bottom with a ¼-inch layer of gelatin mixture. Place in refrigerator to set.

4 When gelatin in oval dish is set, remove from refrigerator and assemble in this way: arrange olives cut side down in 2 lines, about 1¼ inches apart, down the center of the dish. Next arrange the meat pieces over the olives and set the asparagus spears so they overhang the meat; alternate the directions of the spear ends so that one points to the right, the next to the left, the next to the right and so on. Place a shallot in each opening between asparagus spears and stalks (shallots should rest on the thin layer of set gelatin). Then arrange beets, carrots, mushrooms, and parsley so each will show through the gelatin when it is set and turned out. Add these vegetables along the outer edge of the dish, all the way round.

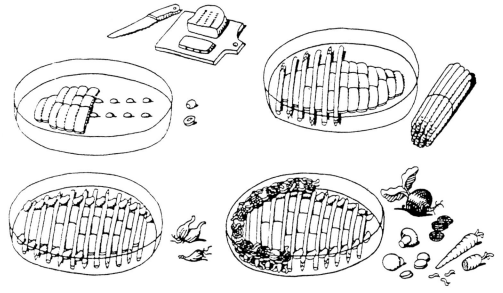

5 Ladle or spoon remaining gelatin (easiest if it is cold and syrupy) over the arrangement of vegetables and meat most carefully; do not disturb arrangement. Cover dish with plastic wrap and refrigerate until set, several hours or, better still, overnight.

6 To unmold, loosen edge a bit with small flexible knife and immerse dish in hot water for a few seconds at a time until mold begins to loosen. Turn out on large oval silver tray or white platter, as either will show off the colors to best advantage. Serve with Horseradish Cream Sauce, page 264.

Circles of Endive Mold

SERVES 8

A fantasy to behold. Fresh vegetables with a dollop of gorgonzola in a glistening aspic. Use your favorite soft cheese to fill the endive circles, if you wish, and if you can't find radicchio use one of your favorite lettuces, or shredded celery and radishes. See photo 1 opposite page 92.

6 fresh Belgian endives
4 ounces creamy gorgonzola cheese
¼ cup mayonnaise
8 ounces fresh snow peas, blanched
   and cut diagonally into 1-inch pieces
4 carrots, cooked and shredded
1 cup fresh or frozen green peas, cooked
8 to 10 ounces radicchio, washed,
   dried and shredded to make about
   3 cups
½ cup chopped spring onions
salt
freshly ground pepper
2 tablespoons sugar
4 cups rich chicken stock or vegetable
   broth

4 packets (¼ ounce each) unflavored
   gelatin
2 egg shells, crushed
2 egg whites, beaten until foamy

SAUCE
(makes about ¾ cup)
¼ cup olive oil
1 tablespoon white wine vinegar
1 teaspoon sugar
¼ cup mayonnaise
¼ cup sour cream
salt
freshly ground pepper

1 Separate leaves from 3 endives, wash, and dry. Cream gorgonzola and mayonnaise and put some of this mixture on the inside of the leaves. Put leaves of endive together as they were originally, pressing them together somewhat firmly but without allowing cheese mixture to ooze out. Refrigerate for 30 minutes or longer. When endives are firm enough to slice, cut slices ⅓ inch thick. Lay flat on a plate and refrigerate until ready to use.

2 Prepare other vegetables as described above, adding salt and pepper as you wish. Shred the remaining 3 endives by hand or in processor and combine with the shredded radicchio and onion. Toss both with 2 tablespoons sugar, salt, and pepper.

3 Combine broth, gelatin, and egg shells in a saucepan. Add egg whites to top, covering all the liquid (do this with a rubber spatula, as if you were covering a meringue pie). Bring to a boil, lower heat immediately and simmer undisturbed for 15 minutes; do *not* stir. Egg whites will look cooked and may split open, but don't fret. Pour mixture through 2 layers of cheesecloth arranged in a strainer over a bowl large enough to hold the liquid. Squeeze cheesecloth to extract clear liquid, but don't squeeze too hard or cooked egg white will come through. Cool before using in mold.

4 Lightly oil a 2-quart charlotte mold and refrigerate it. Pour enough aspic into cold mold to come ⅓ inch up the sides. Refrigerate and allow to set (it will set rapidly if mold is very cold). When set, arrange circles of cheese-filled endive inside mold on top of aspic, allowing approximately ½ inch between circles. Arrange some pieces of snow peas between circles, overlapping some of the endive. Carefully spoon more aspic over circles barely to cover them. Allow aspic to set in refrigerator.

5 Add the shredded carrots and more aspic; allow to set. Add green peas and more snow peas, then more aspic just to cover; let set. Spoon some aspic over remaining endive circles and let aspic set.

6 Pile radicchio and onion mixture in center of mold. Arrange remaining circles of endive against sides of mold with aspic side touching mold. Push radicchio mixture against circles to hold in place. Pour remaining aspic into mold and refrigerate until set; aspic should reach top of mold.

7 To make the sauce, mix all ingredients and blend until smooth. If thinner sauce is desired, thin with light cream. Serve with mold.

Broccoli Flan with Mussel Ragout

❧

SERVES 2

2½ pounds fresh mussels, scrubbed and debearded
1 tablespoon butter
½ cup finely chopped celery (about 1 stalk)
1 large shallot, finely chopped
¼ cup dry white wine
¼ cup water

12 ounces fresh broccoli, trimmed
1 egg, room temperature
¼ cup whipping cream
¼ teaspoon freshly grated nutmeg
salt
freshly ground pepper
2 tablespoons whipping cream
3 tablespoons chilled butter

1 Combine mussels in large bowl with enough ice water to cover. Let stand at least 1 hour or refrigerate in water overnight. Discard any mussels that float to the top, break or open.

2 Melt 1 tablespoon butter in large saucepan over medium-high heat. Add celery and shallot and stir until softened, 2 to 3 minutes. Add wine, water and mussels and bring to boil. Cover immediately and cook until mussels open, about 5 minutes, shaking pot frequently. Remove mussels from pot using slotted spoon; discard any that are not open. Strain broth through strainer lined with 2 layers of moistened cheesecloth set over large bowl. Discard shells; add mussels to broth. Set aside.

3 Bring large amount of salted water to rapid boil in large saucepan over high heat. Peel broccoli stalks and cut into 1-inch pieces; cut flowerets into 1-inch pieces. Add all broccoli to pan and cook until just crisp-tender, about 5 minutes. Drain well. Pat dry with paper towels. Cut broccoli into ¼-inch dice.

4 Preheat oven to 350°F. Liberally butter four 6-ounce molds or custard cups. Line bottoms of molds with buttered parchment paper. Mix egg, ¼ cup cream and nutmeg with salt and pepper in small bowl. Puree 2½ cups diced broccoli in processor or blender until smooth. Blend in egg mixture. Taste and adjust seasoning. Spoon broccoli mixture evenly into prepared molds. Arrange molds in roasting pan. Add enough boiling water to pan to come ⅔ up sides of molds. Bake until tester inserted in center comes out clean, about 1 hour; if tops begin to brown, cover molds with foil. Remove from oven and set aside while preparing sauce.

5 Drain mussel broth through strainer set over medium saucepan. Place saucepan over medium-high heat and cook until broth is reduced by half. Blend in 2 tablespoons cream. Whisk in butter 1 tablespoon at a time. Add mussels and just warm through; do not boil or cook further or mussels will toughen. Unmold flans onto individual plates. Spoon mussels and sauce evenly around flans. Serve immediately.

Parmesan Potatoes in a Charlotte Mold

SERVES 4 TO 6

These potatoes with ham and cheese make an outstanding entree; the presentation is spectacular. Just add a colorful salad.

8 medium-size baking potatoes, whole
   and unpeeled
1 tablespoon shortening
2 tablespoons salt
10 tablespoons (1¼ sticks) butter
4 large onions, finely chopped

1 cup finely diced ham
½ cup whipping cream
½ cup sour cream
1 teaspoon paprika
½ cup freshly grated Parmesan cheese
salt

1 With your hands, rub the shortening over the potatoes. Sprinkle the potatoes all over with salt and place them in a pie plate or another baking pan. Cover with a sheet of foil and bake in preheated 400°F oven for 1 to 1¼ hours, or until tender; test for doneness by piercing the largest potato with a knife or fork.

2 While the potatoes are baking, add 2 tablespoons butter and the chopped onions to a large skillet or saucepan. Cook them slowly until they just begin to turn color, about 10 minutes; do not scorch the onions or they will make unsightly specks in the potato mold. Set the onions aside.

3 Remove the potatoes from the oven. Holding one side of each with a potholder, cut the potato in half lengthwise and scoop out as much of the flesh as you can (or just peel them; either method seems to work easily). Put the potato pulp in a baking dish and mash it well with 6 tablespoons (¾ stick) butter. Season with salt and keep warm. If mixture cools, set the baking pan in the oven to warm it up again.

4 Grease a 1½-quart charlotte mold with the remaining 2 tablespoons butter (use the full 2 tablespoons). Fill ⅓ of the mold with some of the warm potato mixture, packing it tightly into the mold. (The best way to do

this is to press down on the mixture with your fingers, but you can also use a rubber spatula or wooden spoon.) Arrange a layer of about ⅓ of the cooked onions on top of the potatoes. Do the same with the ham. Add another layer of potatoes, filling the mold ⅔ full. Add another layer of onions and ham. Repeat the procedure with the remaining potatoes, onions and ham, making a third triple layer. Place the mold in a preheated 350°F oven and leave it there for 5 minutes, just until the butter used for greasing the mold melts.

5 While the mold is in the oven, combine the creams, scald them, add the paprika, and mix well with a whisk. Remove the mold from the oven and run a knife inside the rim to help loosen the potatoes. Turn the mold out onto an ovenproof platter. Pour the cream over the mold; some of it will run down the sides. Sprinkle Parmesan cheese over the entire mold; be sure to get Parmesan on the sides. Run the mold under the broiler for several minutes to melt the cheese before serving.

Zucchini and Leek Darioles

SERVES 8

A *dariole* is a small soufflé baking dish about 3½ inches wide and 1½ inches deep. It is most frequently used for individual chocolate and other dessert soufflés, but is also ideal for main course preparations such as this one — a custardlike mousse with the delicate zucchini-leek flavor.

1½ pounds fresh zucchini
1 medium-size leek, 1 × 6 inches
2 eggs
1 egg white
6 tablespoons crème fraîche
salt
freshly ground pepper
2 tablespoons butter

TO ASSEMBLE
8 lettuce leaves, washed and dried

2 medium leeks, 1 × 6 inches
2 medium zucchini, 1 × 6 inches
1 tablespoon butter
⅓ cup vegetable or olive oil
juice of 1 lemon
1 teaspoon sugar
salt
freshly ground pepper
8 watercress sprigs, washed and dried
½ cup crème fraîche

1 Wash the zucchini and trim ends, but do not peel. Cut into 1-inch pieces. Wash leek carefully and cut away tough green part. Cut leek into ¼-inch slices. Place zucchini and leek in a saucepan and add water barely to cover. Bring to boil, lower heat, cover and cook for about 20 minutes or until tender. Drain in a colander or large strainer, pressing down on vegetables to extract as much liquid as possible. Puree in a food processor or blender; you should have approximately 2 cups puree.

2 In a large bowl combine eggs, egg white, crème fraîche, salt, and pepper and blend well. Add puree and mix thoroughly. Taste and adjust seasoning. Butter 8 small soufflé dishes (darioles) and divide zucchini mixture among them. Put the soufflé dishes in a baking pan and add hot water to the pan to come halfway up sides of soufflé dishes. Bake in preheated 300°F oven for 50 minutes until mousse is set. Test with a knife blade — if it comes out clean, molds are set.

3 While darioles are baking, prepare for the assembly by washing leeks and zucchini as above, but cut them into ½-inch-thick slices. Heat the butter and 1 tablespoon of the oil in a large skillet and sauté the leek and zucchini slices on both sides. Keep the leek slices intact by turning carefully; both vegetables should brown a little, especially the zucchini. When done (you may have to sauté in batches), transfer to a large, flat platter.

4 Mix remaining oil with lemon juice and sugar. Season the vegetable slices with salt and pepper and pour the lemon juice mixture overall.

5 Arrange a lettuce leaf on each plate and turn out a dariole onto center of each leaf. Divide the sautéed zucchini and leeks among the 8 plates, spooning the sauce over the sautéed vegetables and the darioles. Garnish each dariole by placing a watercress sprig alongside. Top each dariole with ½ teaspoon crème fraîche.

Water Chestnuts, Spring Onions, Oranges, and Duck in Aspic

SERVES 6

2 whole 4-pound dressed ducks
salt and freshly ground pepper
1 tablespoon paprika
2 garlic cloves, halved
2 whole onions, each stuck with a clove
2 unpeeled oranges, quartered
3 tablespoons butter
1 cup fresh orange juice
½ cup orange liqueur

STOCK
Bones and giblets from both ducks
2 carrots, coarsely chopped
1 celery stalk with leaves, coarsely
  chopped
1 onion, coarsely chopped
2 parsley sprigs (with stems)

salt
several peppercorns
1 cup dry white wine
2 quarts water
2 egg whites (reserve shells)

TO ASSEMBLE
3 oranges, skin and pith completely
  removed, thinly sliced (remove seeds
  if necessary)
2 cups thinly sliced water chestnuts
5 cups thinly sliced green onions
¼ cup chopped fresh parsley
½ cup orange liqueur
1½ quarts clarified duck stock
3 packets (¼ ounce each) unflavored
  gelatin
roasted duck pieces

1 Wash ducks in cool water; dry inside and out. Season cavities with salt, pepper, and paprika. Stuff each with garlic, onion, and orange. Add 1 tablespoon butter to each. Rub outsides with remaining butter, salt, and pepper, and place breast down on rack in roasting pan. Prick skin to release fat. Pour ¼ cup orange juice into pan.

2 Roast ducks in preheated 350°F oven for 2 hours, basting with orange juice and liqueur every 15 minutes. After 45 minutes, turn ducks breast side up. Remove fat as you roast. Cut meat from ducks in as large pieces as you can. Set meat aside, reserving bones and carcass for stock. Include browned pieces of skin.

3 Combine stock ingredients, bring to boil, reduce heat and simmer, partially covered, for 3 hours. (Note: you will need 1½ quarts of stock; if it cooks down too much, cover pan completely.) Strain stock, extracting as much liquid as possible. Discard bones and vegetables. Refrigerate overnight and remove congealed fat. To clarify stock, beat egg whites until they form soft peaks, crush the shells with your hands, and add broth to the stock. Bring mixture to a boil, whisking constantly. Stop whisking, turn the heat as low as possible, and cook 10 to 15 minutes. The egg whites will become meringuelike, while fat and particles will be trapped. Strain stock carefully through several layers of cheesecloth.

4 To assemble, marinate oranges, water chestnuts, green onions, and parsley in orange liqueur for several hours or overnight. In a medium saucepan, heat duck stock with gelatin just until gelatin is dissolved. Remove from heat and pour a thin layer into an oiled 9½ × 14 × 2¼-inch oval glass dish. Let set in refrigerator. Chill remaining aspic just until slightly thickened.

5 Arrange orange slices on set layer of aspic. Fill empty spaces with parsley and spring onions. Place duck pieces, water chestnuts, remaining onions, and parsley into dish. Pour or spoon aspic carefully overall. Chill until aspic is completely set, several hours or overnight. Run knife around edge of dish and immerse dish very briefly in hot water to release mold. Unmold onto large oval platter. Garnish with additional orange slices, water chestnuts, green onions.

A Mold of Zucchini with Special Vegetable Fillings

SERVES 6

This is a lovely, easy-to-make, fresh mold that can be filled with many things. We present it with fresh asparagus spears bathed in hollandaise sauce, but you can steam broccoli or cauliflower flowerets and bathe either in a cheese sauce, or fill the mold with mushrooms sautéed in butter and sprinkled with bacon bits. See photo 1 following page 172.

2 to 2½ pounds fresh zucchini (4 cups grated)
salt
8 ounces mushrooms
1 tablespoon butter
1 tablespoon olive oil
¼ cup finely chopped onion
freshly ground pepper
4 eggs
2 egg yolks
½ cup whipping cream
½ cup fine fresh breadcrumbs

½ cup freshly grated Parmesan cheese
2 tablespoons chopped fresh basil or
   1 teaspoon dried
1 tablespoon chopped fresh oregano or
   1 teaspoon dried
4 tablespoons (½ stick) butter, melted
   and cooled
1 pound asparagus, trimmed, cut into
   1½-inch lengths, cooked until
   tender, drained, and patted dry
Hollandaise Sauce (page 254)

1 Buy or pick small, fresh zucchini. Wash and dry the whole zucchini and cut off the ends; do not peel. If the zucchini are tiny, grate them in their entirety; if they are larger, cut them in half lengthwise, scoop out the seeds, and then grate. Put the grated zucchini in a colander, add a little salt and let stand at least 30 minutes to drain off as much liquid as possible. Squeeze dry in a cloth towel to remove excess liquid.

2 Wipe mushrooms with a moistened cloth or paper towel. Cut off about half of each stem (freeze these stem pieces for stockpot use). Chop the mushrooms and squeeze dry by wringing them in a cloth towel.

3 Heat the butter and oil in a skillet and sauté the mushrooms and onion until almost dry. Add salt and pepper and set aside.

4 Combine zucchini and mushroom mixture in a large bowl and mix well.

5 Beat the eggs and egg yolks together. Pour in the cream and mix well. Add the breadcrumbs, Parmesan cheese, basil, oregano, and the cooled melted butter. Stir in zucchini mixture. Taste and adjust seasoning.

6 Pour into a generously buttered 1½-quart ring mold. Place the mold in a larger pan and fill it with enough hot water to reach halfway up the sides of the ring mold. Put in a preheated 325°F oven and bake until the mold is set, about 45 to 50 minutes.

7 Remove the ring mold from the pan of water and run a knife around the inside. Place the serving platter over the ring mold and invert to unmold.

8 Fill center of zucchini mold with asparagus pieces. Pass sauce separately. To serve, cut a 2-inch width of mold and add several asparagus lengths to plate. Spoon 2 tablespoons sauce onto plate, not over the mold or asparagus.

Individual Vegetable Timbales: Onion and Eggplant

SERVES 4

ONION TIMBALES
2 tablespoons unsalted butter
12 ounces white onions, very thinly
   sliced (about 2 cups)
2 eggs
½ cup light cream
pinch of freshly grated nutmeg
salt
freshly ground pepper
3 slices boiled ham, prosciutto, or
   Virginia ham, cut into 12 ½ ×
   4-inch strips and four 1-inch disks

EGGPLANT TIMBALES
1 eggplant (1 pound)
2 teaspoons salt
½ cup vegetable oil
1 garlic clove
3 eggs
½ cup whipping cream
Light Tomato Sauce (page 257)

1 To make the onion timbales, melt butter in a medium to large skillet and cook onion slices, stirring frequently until they become transparent and start to turn golden, about 10 minutes. Transfer to a dish or bowl and let cool.

2 In a bowl combine eggs, cream, nutmeg, salt, and pepper and whisk until well combined. When onions are cooled, add to egg mixture. Taste and adjust seasoning. Transfer to 2-cup measure with a spout.

3 Liberally butter four ½-cup timbale cups with flat bottoms. Place a ham disk in bottom of each mold. Arrange strips of ham, equally spaced, running up sides of mold and overlapping onto disk. Pour onion mixture into molds, cover, and set aside.

4 To make the eggplant timbales, wash and dry the eggplant; cut off stem and bottom ends. Stand eggplant upright and with a long, thin, flexible knife, remove the skin in very thin slivers (as thin as you can make them) about 1½ inches wide. Reserve strips of skin. Lay skinned eggplant on its side and cut into ¼-inch slices. Salt slices, put them in a colander, and allow to sit for 30 to 60 minutes. In the meantime, blanch the skins in boiling water for 2 minutes, drain, pat dry and set aside.

5 Place ¼ cup or so of oil in a large skillet and sauté eggplant slices until brown on both sides. Transfer cooked slices to paper toweling to drain.

6 When all slices are cooked, puree them in food processor with the garlic. Add the eggs and cream and process until all is well blended. Taste and adjust seasoning. Transfer mixture to a 2-cup measure with a spout.

7 Liberally butter four ½-cup timbale cups with flat bottoms. From 1 or 2 blanched skins cut four 1-inch circles and set bottom of each in mold, purple side down. Pour eggplant mixture into each cup.

8 Arrange onion and eggplant timbales in roasting pan and add hot water to come halfway up sides of molds. Bake in preheated 375°F oven for 40 minutes. When set, remove from oven and water bath and let stand 5 to 10 minutes before unmolding.

9 Sauté remaining eggplant skins until tender, just a minute or two on each side. Cool. Cut the full length of strip ¾ inch wide. Make a fancy edge on one side of band. When eggplant molds are turned out, wrap each base with an eggplant strip, fancy edge up. Set one of each timbale on each serving plate. Spoon sauce around bases of molds.

Vegetables in an Eggplant Mold

❦

SERVES 6 TO 8

These ingredients go well together, especially when encased and baked in a mold of cooked eggplant slices.

1 eggplant (about 1 pound)
salt
vegetable oil for deep frying
1½ cups Tomato Vegetable Sauce
   (page 258)
2 red bell peppers, cored, seeded, and
   cut into 1-inch squares (about 2 cups)
4 eggs, hard-cooked, peeled, and
   coarsely chopped

8 ounces fontina cheese, cut into
   ¼-inch cubes
freshly ground pepper
3 tablespoons freshly grated Parmesan
   cheese
2 tablespoons unsalted butter

1 Cut off the top and bottom ends of the eggplant; it should be able to sit upright. Do not peel. Slice lengthwise into very thin slices. Reserve the first thin slice (which is totally unpeeled on one side). Cut a 2-inch circle from this piece and prepare it as you do all remaining slices. (This circular piece will serve as a "button" on top of the completed mold.) Freely salt each slice and lay in a colander to drain for 1 hour. Pat each slice dry and set aside.

2 Heat about 3 inches of the vegetable oil in a deep fryer until hot enough to fry eggplant slices, about 375°F. Deep fry several at a time until golden brown, about 1½ minutes per side. When done, remove with tongs to paper toweling to drain.

3 Preheat oven to 375°F. In a large bowl combine the tomato vegetable sauce, red peppers, eggs, fontina cheese and salt and pepper to taste. Set aside.

4 Liberally butter a 2-quart ceramic soufflé dish and line it with about ¾ of the eggplant slices (the slices will extend slightly over the edge of the soufflé dish and must overlap each other). With a large spoon transfer the vegetable mixture to the soufflé dish. Cover with the ends of the eggplant slices. Add the remaining slices, including the "button." Sprinkle the Parmesan over the top and dot overall with butter. Bake until heated through, 30 minutes. This mold may be turned out, and it will be especially attractive if you do. Let it cool for 10 to 15 minutes, then run a sharp knife around edge to loosen mold before turning out. If you do unmold it, move the "button" to the top of the turned-out mold. Sprinkle with additional Parmesan and run under broiler just for a minute or two.

Celery and Carrot in a Round Mold

❦

SERVES 6

6 tablespoons (¾ stick) unsalted butter
4 to 5 carrots, coarsely grated (3 cups)
¼ cup thinly sliced green onions
½ teaspoon celery seed
½ cup grated Gruyère cheese
4 eggs, at room temperature
1 teaspoon Dijon mustard

salt and freshly ground pepper
1½ pounds celery with some leaves,
    finely chopped
3 tablespoons all-purpose flour
1 cup milk
6 tablespoons fresh breadcrumbs

1 In a large saucepan melt 2 tablespoons butter. Sauté the carrots, green onions and celery seed for 2 to 3 minutes. Add ¼ cup of the Gruyère, 2 beaten eggs, mustard, salt, and pepper. Mix and set aside.

2 In another large saucepan melt 2 tablespoons butter and sauté the celery for 3 to 4 minutes. Add the remaining ¼ cup Gruyère.

3 In a small saucepan melt the remaining 2 tablespoons butter, add the flour and stir together thoroughly. Add milk and whisk constantly until the sauce comes to a boil and is thick and smooth.

4 Combine the sauce with the celery mixture, 2 beaten eggs, 5 tablespoons breadcrumbs, salt, and pepper. Mix thoroughly. Taste and adjust seasoning.

5 Preheat oven to 375°F. Butter a 2-quart round soufflé dish. Spread ¼ of the carrot mixture evenly in bottom of dish. Top with ¼ of the celery mixture. Repeat layers until you have used all of both mixtures, ending with the carrot. Sprinkle the remaining 1 tablespoon breadcrumbs over-all. Bake 1 hour. Let rest for 15 minutes before unmolding. Run knife around edge and unmold onto a serving platter. Slice as you would a cake or pie. This is also good cold. Slice and sauté briefly in butter; serve with fresh tomato slices.

❦

Opposite: Vegetable and Pork Filling in Phyllo
(page 110).
Following page: Red Cabbage and Chestnuts,
Sweet and Sour (page 183).

Corn Pudding Baked in Collard Greens

SERVES 6

This corn pudding is great by itself and even better encased in a collard green container.

15 medium-size whole collard leaves
3 eggs
1/4 cup all-purpose flour
1 teaspoon salt
1/2 teaspoon white pepper
2 tablespoons unsalted butter, melted
1/2 cup thinly sliced green onions
1 cup light cream

1 1/2 cups fresh corn kernels (6 ears
   fresh corn) or one 10-ounce package
   frozen corn kernels, thawed, or one
   12-ounce can
pinch of freshly grated nutmeg
1 tablespoon finely chopped fresh
   tarragon or 1 teaspoon dried

1 Wash the collard leaves, leaving them whole but cutting out the stems (it's easiest to do this with scissors). Steam for 4 minutes; the leaves will turn bright green and become pliable. An excellent and easy way to steam them is in a bamboo steamer, the leaves still wet from washing. Remove from steamer, pat dry and set aside.

2 Beat eggs well in a large bowl. Add flour, salt, pepper, butter, green onions and cream and mix well. Add corn, nutmeg and tarragon. Taste and adjust seasoning. Set aside.

3 Liberally butter a springform pan approximately 8 × 4 inches. Arrange collard leaves on bottom and sides of pan, leaving enough overhang and some extra leaves to cover top. Pour corn mixture into pan, enclose with leaves, set pan in larger pan and fill with hot water to come halfway up sides of springform. Place in preheated 375°F oven and bake for about 1 hour or until mold is set. (Test for doneness by inserting sharp knife; if liquid appears on knife or mold is still unset, bake longer.) Allow to sit for 10 minutes or so after removing from oven. Undo springform and serve.

Opposite: Potato Salad with Smoked Salmon (page 201).
Preceding page: A Tart of Six Vegetables (page 90).

Carrots in a Charlotte Mold

❦

SERVES 6

Colorful vegetables and Ribier grapes are set in a rich aspic and served with a spicy horseradish cream sauce.

6 cups chicken stock or vegetable broth
1 celery stalk with leaves, cut into
    ½-inch pieces
2 green onions (including tops), cut
    into ½-inch pieces
6 parsley sprigs (with stems)
1 medium tomato, cored and coarsely
    chopped
1 tablespoon chopped fresh tarragon or
    1 teaspoon dried
3 egg shells, broken into 1 or 2 pieces
3 egg whites, beaten until stiff but not
    dry
3 packets (¼ ounce each) unflavored
    gelatin
6 carrots, cooked and thinly sliced on
    the diagonal
8 ounces Ribier grapes, washed,
    halved, and seeded
4 beets, cooked, sliced as thinly as
    possible, and marinated in ½ cup
    Oil and Vinegar Dressing (page
    261) for 30 minutes
1 small head or wedge red cabbage
    (6 to 8 ounces), sliced ¼ inch thick
    or less (slice by hand, or use
    shredding blade of processor)

1 large purple onion, cut into ¼-inch
    cubes
2 tablespoons sugar
salt
freshly ground pepper

GARNISH
4-ounce bunch Ribier grapes, washed
2 parsley sprigs (with stems)

HORSERADISH SAUCE
(makes about 2 cups)
¼ cup prepared horseradish
2 tablespoons Dijon mustard
4 green onions (including tender green
    parts), finely chopped
2 tablespoons white wine vinegar
1 cup sour cream
½ cup (about) chicken stock or
    vegetable broth
salt
freshly ground pepper

1 To prepare aspic, combine stock or broth with celery, green onions, parsley, tomato, tarragon and egg shells in a saucepan. Using a rubber spatula, spread egg whites on top to cover mixture completely. Bring to a boil, lower heat and simmer gently for 30 minutes; do *not* stir. (The egg whites will harden and may split. Don't fret; just keep stock at a slow simmer.) Pour through strainer lined with several layers of cheesecloth and set over a large bowl.

2 Add gelatin to hot liquid and stir until gelatin is completely dissolved; this may take up to 5 minutes. Place mixture in refrigerator just until slightly thickened.

3 Lightly oil a 2-quart mold with vegetable oil. Pour in aspic to make a layer ¼ inch to ½ inch deep. Refrigerate mold until aspic is set. Season vegetables with salt and pepper. Arrange a circle of overlapping carrot slices 1 inch from the outside of the mold. Inside the carrot circle arrange grape halves, some with cut side facing down and some the other way. Arrange some of the beet slices over the carrots, overlapping carrots by ½ inch. Pour in more aspic to cover carrots, grapes and beets completely. Return to refrigerator and let set.

4 Mix together red cabbage, onion, sugar and salt and pepper. Layer mixture next in the mold, using about half of it. Top with a layer of beets, then add remaining cabbage and onion mixture. Pour in more aspic to cover and return to refrigerator to set.

5 Add a final layer of carrots interspersed with grape halves. Fill with remaining aspic and let set.

6 The simplest and most effective presentation is to turn out the mold, garnish with parsley and place small clusters of grapes on top of parsley.

7 To prepare sauce, combine all ingredients except broth and blend well.

8 Add enough broth to thin to desired consistency. Refrigerate until ready to use. Stir well before serving.

Charlotte Mold Escarole with Brussels Sprout Topping

SERVES 6

Lots of fresh vegetables, dotted with pecans and currants and baked in a mold.

1 pound fresh Brussels sprouts
12 tablespoons (1½ sticks) unsalted
    butter, softened
2½ pounds escarole
8 eggs
⅓ cup whipping cream
salt

freshly ground pepper
pinch of freshly grated nutmeg
¾ cup chopped pecans
½ cup dried currants, steeped in warm
    water for 30 minutes and drained
¼ cup freshly grated Parmesan cheese
1 cup Hollandaise Sauce (page 254)

1 Pick over Brussels sprouts, removing bruised leaves. Make a criss-cross cut in the stem ends and put in cold salted water for 30 minutes. Drain, rinse again in cool water and boil sprouts until barely tender (they will cook again, so they should be a bit underdone). Drain, pat dry and cut them in half crosswise. Melt 1 tablespoon butter in a skillet and sauté sprout halves, cut side down, for a minute or two to give them a little color. Remove from heat and set aside.

2 Pick over escarole, wash thoroughly and cook in boiling salted water until tender. Squeeze out as much liquid as you can (you should have approximately 2 cups). Puree in a food processor or put through a food mill.

3 Beat eggs well, add the cream and blend. Add all remaining butter, reserving enough to butter the mold. Add the pureed escarole, nuts and currants. Season with salt, pepper, and nutmeg. Butter both sides of a circle of parchment or waxed paper to fit bottom of mold.

4 Arrange Brussels sprout halves cut side down on the waxed paper in buttered 2-quart charlotte mold, placing them as close together as you can. Pour in escarole mixture. Place the mold in a larger pan and add enough hot water to come halfway up sides of mold. Bake in a preheated 375°F oven for about 1½ hours, or until mold is firm to the touch and a wooden skewer comes out dry.

5 Remove from oven, run knife around edge of mold and turn out onto ovenproof platter. Remove paper. Sprinkle Parmesan on top and sides and run mold under the broiler for a minute or two until golden. Serve by cutting into wedges and spooning hollandaise at side of each serving.

4

LOAVES, PÂTÉS, AND TERRINES

Loaves, pâtés and terrines can be exotic vegetable preparations. They sound difficult to make, but they aren't really that complicated when you consider how festive and elegant they can be, let alone their versatility as lunch or supper entrees, exciting buffet centerpieces, or chic and tasty picnic fare.

If you like to entertain, these loaves, pâtés and terrines can be of great use to you, especially because they can be made ahead. As main courses, they should be served with salads or another *hot* vegetable. Use cheeses and interesting breads with these dishes to fill out the menu.

Loaf pans are usually measured by length, width and depth — in that order. You can always figure out the volume of the pan by filling it with water, but be sure to fill the pan to the brim. The two-quart loaf pan (commonly called the "standard 8-cup") measures nine inches long, five inches wide and three inches deep. Most of the following recipes call for this size pan or terrine. However, there is also a narrower and longer pan measuring 12 to 14 inches long by 3½ to 4½ inches wide by two to three inches deep. We prefer this size because the terrine will *look* better, and then too, it cuts a smaller slice. If you cut these smaller slices slightly thicker they are easier to serve.

Not all of these loaves are served cold from the refrigerator. Many should be served at room temperature for fullest flavor — for example, the Broccoli, Mushroom and Pine Nut Terrine.

Remember, you can make these today and serve them tomorrow or the day after, or even a few days after that.

Broccoli, Mushroom, and Pine Nut Terrine

SERVES 8

2 tablespoons butter
2 tablespoons olive or vegetable oil
½ cup finely chopped green onions
1 garlic clove, finely chopped
1 pound mushrooms, coarsely chopped
2 tablespoons finely chopped fresh
  orange zest
1 teaspoon dried summer savory
2 teaspoons salt

freshly ground pepper
2 cups finely chopped cooked broccoli,
  drained
1 cup toasted pine nuts
1 cup ricotta
2 eggs
½ cup finely chopped fresh parsley
⅓ teaspoon freshly grated nutmeg

1 Heat butter and oil in a skillet and cook green onions until they wilt and just begin to turn color, 3 to 4 minutes. Add the garlic and mushrooms and cook 5 minutes more, stirring every now and then. Add orange zest, summer savory, salt, and pepper and cook several minutes longer until there is little or no liquid remaining. Transfer mixture to a large bowl and fold in broccoli and pine nuts.

2 Whip ricotta until smooth, add eggs, parsley, and nutmeg and beat until all is combined (this may be done in food processor). Fold into broccoli mixture. Taste and adjust seasoning.

3 Butter a 1-quart terrine or loaf pan and line it with parchment, waxed or brown paper. (Cut paper to fit width and length of pan, making sure paper is long enough in both directions to overlap filling.) Butter paper. Fill pan with the broccoli mixture, spreading it smooth. Cover top with a double thickness of foil.

4 Put pan into another baking pan. Fill larger pan with enough hot water to reach halfway up sides of terrine. Bake for 1½ hours in a preheated 375°F oven. Remove from oven and let come to room temperature, about an hour or so. Remove foil, lift up top paper, and run knife around edges of terrine to loosen it. Invert onto large serving platter and remove remaining paper.

Celery and White Bean Pâté

SERVES 4 TO 6

2 celery hearts with leaves, each about
  1½ × 8 inches
6 tablespoons (¾ stick) butter
3 cups cooked white beans, fresh or
  canned (two 20-ounce cans)
2 eggs, separated
1 cup fresh breadcrumbs
¼ cup finely chopped fresh celery leaves
⅓ cup chicken stock or vegetable broth
3 green onions (including tender green
  parts), thinly sliced

2 garlic cloves, minced
1 teaspoon chopped fresh thyme or
  ½ teaspoon dried
1 teaspoon chopped fresh chervil or
  ½ teaspoon dried
2 teaspoons chopped fresh parsley
salt
freshly ground pepper
1 cup Light Tomato Sauce (page 257)

1 Steam the celery hearts until tender. Separate the 2 or 3 larger stalks from the hearts. Dry them and sauté in 1 tablespoon butter until they turn light golden. Set aside.

2 Puree the beans in a food mill and transfer them to a large bowl. Mix in the egg yolks. Combine the breadcrumbs, celery leaves, and stock or broth and blend with the bean mixture. Beat egg whites until fairly stiff but not dry and fold in.

3 Melt 2 tablespoons butter in a skillet and sauté the green onions, garlic, thyme, chervil, and parsley for 2 minutes. Add salt and pepper and blend into bean mixture. Taste and adjust seasoning.

4 Butter a 1½-quart terrine or loaf pan (about 8 × 4 × 3 inches) using 1 tablespoon butter. Spread about one-half of the bean mixture into the terrine and pat it down with your hand or rubber spatula. Lay the celery hearts and stalks on top after cutting off any remaining root end; fit in the celery by placing some lengths in one direction with others pointing the other way. Cover with remaining bean mixture and tamp down. Melt remaining butter and pour overall. Cover top tightly with foil and put in larger pan filled with enough hot water to reach halfway up sides of terrine.

5 Bake in a preheated 400°F oven for 1 hour or longer. Remove foil after 45 minutes of baking to brown top. Remove from oven, allow to sit for at least 15 minutes and unmold. Serve in thick slices and spoon tomato sauce alongside of each slice; do not spoon sauce over pâté.

Roman Stripe Pâté

SERVES 8

This pâté combines three somewhat tart vegetables — dandelions, kale, and rutabagas — an unusual threesome, but really delicious to most palates. If you want a sweeter vegetable, substitute butternut squash for the rutabaga in the same amount, following the same cooking procedure; in place of white sugar, use brown.

1 pound dandelion greens
1 pound kale
salt
3 tablespoons butter
1 tablespoon olive oil
1½ cups chopped onions (about
  2 medium)
2 garlic cloves, finely chopped
4 ounces smoked ham, finely chopped
1 tablespoon fresh lemon juice
3 tablespoons sugar
freshly ground pepper

4 cups raw rutabaga cut into ½-inch
  cubes (about 2 pounds)
½ teaspoon freshly grated nutmeg
8 ounces mushrooms
¼ cup dry Madeira or dry Sherry
6 packets (¼ ounce each) unflavored
  gelatin
¼ cup all-purpose flour
1½ cups chicken stock
Uncooked Fresh Tomato Sauce
  (page 259)

1 Wash the dandelion and kale greens separately in cool water by soaking 20 minutes or longer on the first wash, 5 to 10 minutes on the second. Place dandelions in one large saucepan with cover and the kale in a second large covered saucepan (no additional water is necessary, as some water will have clung to the leaves). Add salt, cover, and over moderate heat cook the dandelions for about 12 minutes, the kale for 20. Drain in the same colander and press dry. Dry further in cloth or paper toweling. Puree in 2 batches in food processor and transfer puree to a large mixing bowl.

2 Heat 1 tablespoon butter and the oil in a large skillet. Sauté the onion and garlic until onion becomes transparent. Add ham, toss, and cook 1 minute longer. Mix into greens and add lemon juice, 2 tablespoons sugar, salt, and pepper.

3 Add the rutabaga cubes to boiling salted water and cook for 30 minutes after the water returns to boil. Drain well and puree in 2 batches in food processor. Transfer puree to a bowl and add remaining sugar and nutmeg.

4 Melt 1 tablespoon butter in a skillet and sauté mushrooms for about 5 minutes. Transfer to puree with a slotted spoon. Add Madeira to skillet (along with juices from mushrooms) and deglaze pan. As soon as liquid thickens, transfer to puree. Add salt and pepper to taste and mix well.

5 Mix gelatin and flour and set aside. In a saucepan combine stock and remaining tablespoon butter and bring to boil. Add gelatin mixture, remove from heat and whisk until thoroughly blended. Return pan to heat and return to a boil, whisking all the time. Cook for 1 minute. Place in refrigerator until cool and almost set, or place in freezer for 5 to 10 minutes; remove before gelatin sets firmly.

6 Add half of the almost-set gelatin mixture to the greens and the remaining half to the rutabaga; blend thoroughly into each vegetable.

7 Butter a 4 × 11 × 3-inch pâté pan liberally and spoon in one-half of greens mixture. Tap pan on counter or tabletop to settle. Add one-half the rutabaga, spreading it carefully over greens and rutabaga, tapping pan after each addition. Add remaining half of greens; spread and tap again. Add remaining rutabaga; spread and tap again carefully. Cover pan first with waxed paper, then with foil and secure foil as tightly as you can. Put this pan in a slightly larger one and add enough hot water to come halfway up sides of pâté pan. Bake in preheated 350°F oven for 1½ hours. Remove from water bath and top pâté with weight. Cool to room temperature. Refrigerate overnight.

8 Loosen edges of pâté and turn out onto chilled serving platter. Serve with uncooked tomato sauce. Spoon sauce alongside of each pâté slice; do not cover slice with sauce.

Gazpacho Terrine—A Cold Vegetable Pâté

❧

SERVES 8

This is a three-star dish, dazzling to the eye, delicious to the palate, and easy to prepare. It's an ideal warm-weather entree and would be a glorious addition to the buffet table year-round. See photo 3 following page 220.

2 cucumbers, peeled and seeded; cut one into 1-inch chunks and leave other whole

2 large red or yellow bell peppers, cored and seeded; cut one into 1-inch pieces and leave other whole (see note)

2 medium-size red onions, peeled; cut one into 1-inch pieces, leave other whole

4 stalks celery with leaves, strings removed; cut 2 stalks into 1-inch pieces, leave 2 whole

2 garlic cloves

4 cups canned plum tomatoes (one 2-pound 3-ounce can), including liquid

1/4 cup olive oil

2 tablespoons red wine vinegar

1 tablespoon tomato paste

1 1/2 teaspoons ground cumin

1 teaspoon mild chili powder

1/2 cup chopped fresh mint or 1 teaspoon dried

1 tablespoon sugar

2 teaspoons salt, or to taste

1 cup clarified chicken stock or vegetable broth

3 1/2 packets (1/4 ounce each) unflavored gelatin

1/2 cup dry vermouth

2 tablespoons dry sherry

TO ASSEMBLE

8 thin slices dry French or Italian bread

1 cup Oil and Vinegar Dressing (page 261)

1 ripe avocado, peeled, seeded, cut into 8 strips, and brushed with lemon juice to prevent discoloration

6 parsley sprigs

1 In a food processor combine the chunks or pieces of cucumber, pepper, red onion, celery, and garlic. Process until vegetables are chopped fine. Transfer to a large bowl.

2 To the same bowl add the tomatoes, olive oil, vinegar, and tomato paste. Mix well and put through a food mill in batches. Add cumin, chili powder, mint, sugar, and salt. Taste and adjust seasoning.

3 Combine stock or broth and ½ packet gelatin in the top of a double boiler and heat over boiling water until all gelatin is dissolved. Set aside. Arrange red pepper strips along bottom of lightly oiled 2-quart loaf pan to make 3 or 4 criss-crosses. Carefully ladle gelatin mixture over pepper and onion arrangement and place in refrigerator to set. In the same double boiler top combine vermouth, Sherry, and 3 packets gelatin and let soften for about 10 minutes. Heat over boiling water until gelatin dissolves. Pour into tomato mixture.

4 By hand, finely dice the remaining cucumber, bell pepper, red onion and celery stalks (do not use processor or food mill). Add to tomato mixture. Mix well and pour into loaf pan, being careful not to disturb onion and red pepper arrangement. Refrigerate, covered overnight.

5 Loosen edges of mold with sharp flexible knife and dip pan into hot water for several seconds until mold loosens. Invert on attractive serving platter.

6 Lightly dip both sides of each bread slice in dressing. Arrange moistened bread alongside of mold. Arrange avocado slices around mold and add parsley sprigs as you wish. Serve a piece of bread, one avocado slice and a ½-inch slice of the terrine per person.

NOTE

Reserve 8 very thin red pepper strips and 4 very thin red onion slices for garnish.

Ratatouille Terrine Baked in Green Leaves

SERVES 8

We think this is one of the best preparations in this book. It is as good on the fourth day as on the first.

16 to 20 medium to large whole
  collard leaves
4 small zucchini, 1 × 6 inches each
salt
2 small eggplants, 1 to 1½ pounds total
½ to ¾ cup vegetable oil
2 large onions, coarsely chopped
3 garlic cloves, finely chopped
6 green frying peppers, cored, seeded,
  and thinly sliced
2 cups fresh tomatoes, cored, blanched,
  peeled, seeded, and cut into ½-inch
  cubes, or 2 cups drained canned
  plum tomatoes (one 28-ounce can)

2 tablespoons chopped fresh basil or
  1 teaspoon dried
1 teaspoon fennel seed
leaves from 6 parsley sprigs, finely
  chopped
freshly ground pepper
3 eggs
½ cup milk
2 cups fresh bread cubes with basil,
  oregano, salt, and pepper added, or
  purchased herbed croutons

1 Wash the collard leaves, leaving them whole but cutting out the stems with scissors. Steam for 4 minutes; the leaves will turn bright green and become pliable. (An excellent and easy way to steam them is in a bamboo steamer.) Remove from steamer, pat dry, and set aside.

2 Wash and dry the zucchini. Trim ends but do not peel. Cut lengthwise into thin slices, put in colander, salt them and let drain for 40 minutes.

3 Wash and dry eggplants. Cut off ends but do not peel. Cut eggplants lengthwise into thin slices and place in colander with zucchini. Salt the slices and let drain 30 minutes. Dry zucchini and eggplant slices and set aside.

4 Heat a small amount of oil in a large skillet. Sauté zucchini and eggplant slices, allowing them to brown a little. Transfer to paper toweling to drain.

5 Add a little more oil to the same skillet and sauté the onions for 4 minutes or until they turn soft. Add garlic and cook 1 minute. Add the peppers and sauté 2 minutes. Add tomatoes, basil, fennel, parsley, salt, and pepper and cook 10 minutes until nearly all liquid evaporates. Remove from heat.

6 Arrange collard leaves in buttered 2-quart (13 × 5 × 3½-inch) terrine or loaf pan by overlapping leaves inside pan and allowing enough over-hang on each side to completely encase filling; pan will need about 4 small leaves and 12 large. Put a layer of bread cubes in bottom. Make 3 layers with zucchini, eggplant, and tomato mixture, adding some bread cubes to each layer. Be sure to put some bread cubes in each corner of pan.

7 Beat eggs and milk in bowl. Make knife insertions into layered vegeta-bles to help absorb egg mixture. Slowly and carefully pour egg mixture into mold, a little at a time, until vegetables absorb liquid; continue until all egg is used. Overlap collard leaves and enclose completely; if more leaves are needed, use them. Cover top with a double layer of foil and secure around edge of terrine. Put in a larger baking pan and add enough hot water to come halfway up sides of terrine. Bake in preheated 375°F oven for 1½ hours. Allow to cool 15 minutes before turning out. This may be served warm, at room temperature or cold.

Spinach and Veal Loaf

SERVES 6 TO 8

A classic, simple-to-make loaf of vegetables, herbs, and veal. The Swiss cheese adds a nice flavor.

4 tablespoons (½ stick) unsalted butter
3 tablespoons all-purpose flour
½ cup milk
½ cup whipping cream
½ teaspoon salt
white pepper
pinch of freshly grated nutmeg
1 cup fresh breadcrumbs
¼ cup milk
1 pound ground veal
1 teaspoon finely chopped fresh
  tarragon or ½ teaspoon dried

1 teaspoon finely chopped fresh thyme
  or ½ teaspoon dried
½ cup finely chopped onion
½ cup finely chopped shallots
2 eggs, room temperature
salt
freshly ground pepper
1 pound fresh spinach leaves, cooked,
  drained, and coarsely chopped
  (about 3 cups)
2 cups shredded Swiss cheese

1 In a small saucepan melt 3 tablespoons butter over moderate heat without letting it brown. Remove pan from heat, add the flour and whisk to blend. Add the milk and cream and whisk until smooth. Return the pan to moderate heat and bring to boil, whisking constantly. When white sauce is quite thick and smooth, reduce the heat to its lowest point and simmer the sauce for 2 to 3 minutes to remove any taste of raw flour. Stir in salt, pepper, and nutmeg. Set aside.

2 In a large bowl combine ¾ cup breadcrumbs, milk, veal, tarragon, thyme, and ½ cup of the white sauce. Mix lightly and set aside.

3 In a small saucepan melt 1 tablespoon butter over moderate heat. Sauté the onion and shallots for 2 minutes. Add to veal mixture with 1 egg, salt, and pepper.

4 In a separate bowl combine cooked spinach, remaining ½ cup white sauce, remaining egg, 1 cup Swiss cheese, salt, and pepper. Mix thoroughly.

5 Preheat oven to 375°F. Butter a 9 × 5 × 3-inch loaf pan and add ¾ of the veal mixture, pressing down evenly. Spoon the spinach mixture over the meat, being sure to get into the corners. Spread the remaining veal mixture over. Sprinkle the remaining 1 cup Swiss cheese overall.

6 Bake the loaf for 1 hour; if top is not browned enough, put it under the broiler for a few minutes. Let the loaf rest for 30 minutes or longer before unmolding and serving.

Mosaic Vegetable Terrine

SERVES 6

A very elegant dish. We think it is best made two or three days before serving. See photo 1 opposite page 220.

4 long carrots, quartered lengthwise
  (about 8 ounces)
6 ounces young, tender green beans
10 ounces fresh or frozen green peas
1 large ripe avocado or 2 small ones
juice of ½ lemon
salt
freshly ground pepper
1 pound boned chicken breasts,
  trimmed of all fat
1½ cups rich chicken stock
6 tablespoons fresh lemon juice
2 tablespoons chopped fresh tarragon
  or 1 teaspoon dried

2 tablespoons Dijon mustard
4 tablespoons (½ stick) chilled butter,
  cut into ¼-inch pieces
3 egg whites, chilled
1 cup corn or vegetable oil, or ½ cup
  corn plus ½ cup peanut oil
14 to 16 bottled or canned grape
  leaves, rinsed in cool water several
  times and dried
1 recipe Mayonnaise (page 261),
  mixed with 2 finely chopped green
  onions and several drops of chili oil

1 Cook the cut carrots in boiling salted water for about 6 to 8 minutes, until tender. Drain and refresh under cold water. Cook peas about 1 minute and beans about 5 minutes in same way. Pat vegetables dry, season with salt and pepper and refrigerate.

2 Halve avocado lengthwise, peel, and discard pit. Slice ½-inch thick and coat with juice of ½ lemon. Season with salt and pepper; set aside.

3 Simmer chicken in chicken stock until tender, about 8 minutes. Remove, let cool, and cut into ⅜-inch cubes. Add lemon juice, salt, and pepper and chill thoroughly, about 1 hour. (If you want to speed up chilling process, place chicken in freezer but do not let it freeze.)

4 Chill container of blender or food processor; puree chicken in it. Add tarragon, mustard, and butter and process for 3 or 4 seconds. Add chilled egg whites and blend. Add oil a little at a time, as if you were making mayonnaise (but not quite as slowly). Taste and adjust seasoning. Refrigerate mixture until ready to assemble.

5 Lightly oil terrine measuring about 13 × 4 × 3 inches. Spread grape leaves as attractively as you can on bottom and sides, with enough overhang to enclose entire terrine.

6 Spread a ¼- to ½-inch-thick layer of chicken mousse on leaves. Arrange avocado on mousse in one solid layer. Add more mousse and top with carrots, arranged side by side in one layer. Add more filling, then green peas. Complete terrine by adding any remaining chicken mousse.

7 Fold over grape leaves and cover terrine with a piece of buttered, waxed parchment or brown paper. Set terrine in larger pan and add enough hot water to come halfway up sides of terrine. Bake for 30 minutes in preheated 350°F oven. Remove from oven and let terrine cool in water bath. Refrigerate overnight. Unmold and cut into ¾-inch slices.

8 Put a tablespoon or so of mayonnaise alongside of plate before laying down slice of terrine. Garnish with a sprig of fresh tarragon, mint, watercress, or parsley, or a whole green onion.

5

TARTS AND QUICHES

Tarts as we know them today usually have only a bottom crust. If you glance through old cookbooks, however, "pies" and "tarts" are interchangeable. One thing is sure: tarts have been around a long time. They are mentioned in Chaucer's *Canterbury Tales*, and the very word *torta* dates to early Latin times.

In their *Dictionary of Gastronomy* (McGraw-Hill, 1970) Simon and Howe discuss an amusing theory they found in Kettner's *Book of the Table,* published in 1877. The hypothesis is that our medieval ancestors lacked dinner plates. To solve the problem someone figured out that a crust of bread would serve as a plate. In France, for many years the plate was in fact just that: a *tourte* or *tarte* was the centerpiece of the meal, and a family would finish off dinner by eating its lower crust, the dinner plate. The evidence does suggest, therefore, that the strict meaning (if one were necessary) of *tart* is an open filled crust in the nature of a plate.

Quiche, also of ancient origin, is an open-faced tart. Fillings vary all over the lot, probably the most famous being Quiche Lorraine, made with a rich short pastry holding bacon, eggs, and cream.

Of all the short crust doughs, we find the recipe on page 267 to be the most versatile. It will make enough pastry for two tarts or pies, with enough left for a lattice top; or there is sufficient pastry for two deep-dish preparations. To prevent the fillings from making the crust soggy, cooked vegetables must be drained well and patted dry, and the pastry itself is generally baked before adding the filling. Often the pastry is brushed with egg wash as soon as it is removed from the oven and before it is filled; this, too, helps prevent sogginess.

For best results in making this pastry, adhere to two simple rules: have all ingredients cold and handle dough as little as possible. An electric mixer with a dough paddle arm is a worthwhile investment for blending the dough. Once the pastry ingredients are blended, refrigeration is a must. Wrap dough tightly in waxed paper and put it in the refrigerator — it will be fine for several days. Or freeze it; it will only require overnight thawing before it is rolled.

Tarts and quiches, when prepared properly, are dishes in which the balance of texture and flavor is just right. They look and taste delicious. And contrary to what many people believe, they need little or no meat, nor do they have to be elaborate. With salad and fruit, a tart or quiche makes the ideal vegetable meal.

Vegetable Tart with Gruyère

☙

SERVES 6 TO 8

1 baked 10-inch tart shell (page 267)
vegetable oil
½ cup thinly sliced shallots
½ cup zucchini cut into ½-inch cubes
½ cup snow peas cut diagonally into
   ½-inch slices
1 cup eggplant cut into ½-inch cubes
½ cup mushrooms cut into ¼-inch slices
1 cup peeled potato cut into ½-inch
   cubes

1½ cups shredded Gruyère (about
   5 ounces) — use large holes of hand
   grater, shredder, or processor
2 eggs
2 egg whites
2 cups light cream
½ teaspoon cumin seed
salt
freshly ground pepper

1 Sauté each of the vegetables: begin with 2 tablespoons oil and sauté shallots until they begin to turn golden. Transfer to paper toweling with slotted spoon. Add 1 tablespoon more oil and sauté zucchini until crisp-tender; it should be undercooked. Transfer to paper towel. Sauté snow peas for less than a minute; remove. Add 2 tablespoons oil for eggplant, sauté until crisp, and transfer to paper toweling. Add 2 tablespoons more oil to sauté potato until brown and tender; transfer to toweling. Add mushrooms and sauté until they brown at the edges, then transfer to toweling with slotted spoon. Pat vegetables dry with additional toweling. Transfer all vegetables to bottom of tart shell and spread cheese overall.

2 Whisk eggs, egg whites, cream, cumin, salt, and pepper until well blended and pour over vegetables and cheese.

3 Bake for 1 hour (or longer, if necessary) in preheated 350°F oven. Allow tart to cool for 15 minutes or so before cutting and serving.

4 Decorate with vegetable cutouts blanched in boiling water, as shown in drawing.

Broccoli Rabe Tart

SERVES 8 TO 10

1 recipe Basic Pastry (page 267)
2 pounds broccoli rabe
2 tablespoons olive oil
4 tablespoons (½ stick) butter
2 cups coarsely chopped onions
3 garlic cloves, minced
½ cup finely chopped flat-leaf parsley
4 eggs
½ cup whipping cream

1 teaspoon finely chopped lemon zest
generous pinch of freshly grated nutmeg
salt
freshly ground pepper
8 ounces mascarpone cheese or
   8 ounces cream cheese whipped
   with ¼ cup whipping cream
½ cup toasted pine nuts

1 Roll out dough as directed in recipe for Basic Pastry. Fit about half of dough into 10-inch pie pan. Cut remaining dough into 8 to 10 leaf shapes, about 1 × 2 inches. Bake leaves on cookie sheet just until light brown, about 8 to 10 minutes. Bake pie shell until golden brown, then brush entire surface with 1 egg beaten with 1 tablespoon water. Return to oven and bake 1 minute longer. Let cool.

2 Wash broccoli rabe well and cut off the stem ends. Remove the strings on the larger stalks as you would on a large celery stalk. Cut the larger leaves in half. Immerse stalks and leaves in cool water until ready to cook.

3 Cook broccoli rabe in boiling salted water until almost done. Drain well in colander or large strainer; squeeze dry by pressing with back of large spoon.

4 Heat oil and 2 tablespoons butter in a large skillet and cook onion until it begins to color, about 5 minutes. Add drained broccoli and cook an additional 5 minutes to evaporate moisture. Add garlic and parsley and cook another minute or two. Remove from heat and transfer mixture to a large mixing bowl. Allow to cool for 15 to 20 minutes.

5 In another bowl, whisk eggs, cream, lemon zest, nutmeg, salt, and pepper until thoroughly combined. Add broccoli mixture and blend. Blend in cheese and almost all of the pine nuts (remaining pine nuts will be used to garnish top). Taste and adjust seasoning. Transfer to baked pie shell and dot with remaining butter.

6 Bake for 40 to 45 minutes in preheated 375°F oven. Remove from oven and arrange baked pastry leaves in center, keeping in mind that you'll want to cut around and not through them. (A good guide is to use as many pastry leaves as you plan to cut servings.) Sprinkle remaining pine nuts on top of tart. Serve warm or at room temperature.

A Tart of Six Vegetables

Seven vegetables are included here; choose six you like best.

SERVES 6

See photo 3 following page 60.

5 ounces carrots (about 3), peeled
3 tablespoons butter
1 small onion, finely chopped
2 tablespoons olive oil
5 ounces mushrooms, thinly sliced
1 shallot, finely chopped
salt and freshly ground pepper
2 garlic cloves
8 ounces fresh spinach (stems
  removed), washed, blanched for
  1 minute in boiling water, finely
  chopped, and drained well (1 cup
  tightly packed)
pinch of freshly grated nutmeg
2 cups broccoli (flowerets and tender
  stems), blanched, cut into 1-inch
  pieces, and drained
2 large or 3 medium beets
2 tablespoons vinegar
¼ teaspoon caraway seed
1 bay leaf
2 cloves
3 turnips (the size of large eggs),
  peeled, sliced ¼ inch thick, cooked,
  and cut into julienne

12 asparagus spears (less than ½ inch
  thick)
1 tablespoon fresh lemon juice

PASTRY
1⅓ cups all-purpose flour
1 teaspoon salt
1½ teaspoons sugar
8 tablespoons (1 stick) chilled unsalted
  butter, cut into ¼-inch cubes
1 egg, lightly beaten
2 tablespoons milk
1 egg, lightly beaten (to coat surface of
  baked tart shell)

BECHAMEL-EGG SAUCE
2 tablespoons butter
2 tablespoons all-purpose flour
¾ cup milk, heated to boiling
salt
white pepper to taste
¼ teaspoon freshly grated nutmeg
3 eggs
¾ cup whipping cream
¼ teaspoon Worcestershire sauce

1 In a large mixing bowl combine flour, salt, sugar, and butter for pastry. Blend with fingers, pastry blender, or paddle beater of electric mixer until mixture looks like coarse meal; do not overwork. Add 1 egg and milk and mix quickly. Press dough into a ball and work the dough on a lightly floured surface for only 5 or 6 seconds more. Shape into a disk, wrap in waxed paper, and refrigerate for 1 hour. (Dough can be frozen for several weeks, but add another wrapping.)

2 Roll dough out on lightly floured surface and fit it into a 9-inch quiche pan (1¼ inches deep). Line with foil and fill with rice, dried beans, or pie weights. Allow to rest in refrigerator for 1 hour. Bake in preheated 425°F oven for 15 minutes. Remove from oven; remove foil and weights. Paint inside of shell with beaten egg and return to oven for 2 to 3 minutes, until egg wash is firm. Set aside until ready for assembly.

3 Steam carrots in ½ cup water in covered skillet for 6 minutes. Drain, thinly slice diagonally, and set aside. Pour out water from skillet, dry pan and melt 2 tablespoons butter in it. Add onion and carrot to pan and sauté 3 minutes. Transfer to small bowl and set aside. Heat 1 tablespoon oil. Add mushrooms, shallot, salt, and pepper and sauté 3 minutes over high heat. Drain in strainer and set aside.

4 Melt 1 tablespoon butter and sauté 1 clove garlic until lightly browned. Discard garlic, add spinach and sauté 3 minutes. Add salt, pepper, nutmeg. Transfer spinach to small bowl and set aside. Heat remaining olive oil and sauté other clove of garlic until lightly browned. Discard garlic, add broccoli, and sauté 3 minutes. Season with salt and pepper and drain in strainer. Transfer to small bowl and set aside.

5 Combine beets, vinegar, caraway seed, bay leaf, and cloves in saucepan and add enough water to cover. Bring to a boil, lower heat, and cook until beets are barely done (test by inserting fork or knife; beets should be firm). Remove beets, cool, peel, cut into julienne, transfer to small bowl, set aside.

6 Salt and pepper cooked turnip pieces. Place in small bowl and set aside. Wash and trim asparagus spears; cut diagonally into 1-inch pieces. Blanch in boiling water 2 minutes. Drain and place in small bowl. Toss with salt, pepper, and lemon juice; set aside.

7 For sauce, melt butter in saucepan and bring to boil. Add flour and whisk for 3 minutes over low heat, do not let flour color. Add hot milk and whisk until smooth. Season with salt, white pepper, and nutmeg and simmer for 15 minutes over low heat, stirring frequently. Remove from heat.

8 Combine eggs, cream, and Worcestershire and mix well. Blend into sauce. Arrange 6 of the 7 vegetables in wedges in the tart, resembling 6 pie servings. Fit vegetable pieces as snugly as you can, arranging them attractively on top — for example, save asparagus tips for topping asparagus stalks, and arrange all the points in one direction.

9 Carefully pour sauce over vegetables; do *not* let it run over edge of pastry. Bake for 1 hour in preheated 375°F oven. Let rest 10 to 15 minutes before cutting and serving. To serve, ask who prefers which vegetable and/or slice down center of one vegetable portion and down center of adjoining one to get a pie slice of half one vegetable, half another.

Opposite: Circles of Endive Mold (page 44).

Tomato, Shallot, and Pancetta Tart

SERVES 6 TO 8

1 baked 10-inch deep-dish pie shell
  (page 267)
¼ cup Dijon mustard
⅔ cup finely diced fontina cheese
  (about 6 ounces)
1 tablespoon butter
4 ounces pancetta, cut into ¼-inch cubes
½ cup finely chopped shallots, green
  onions, or onions
½ cup finely chopped zucchini
1 large garlic clove, finely chopped

2 eggs
½ cup light cream
1 cup canned plum tomatoes, drained,
  put through food mill, or squeezed
  by hand to remove seeds, then cut
  into small pieces (do not use
  processor)
1 tablespoon chopped fresh oregano or
  1 teaspoon dried
salt
freshly ground pepper

1 Coat the bottom of the baked pie shell with the mustard and sprinkle with most of the fontina cheese (save just enough cheese to top tart later). Set aside.

2 Melt butter in medium skillet and cook pancetta for 6 to 7 minutes, until it begins to brown, stirring frequently. Add shallots or onions and zucchini and cook until they too begin to turn color, about 5 minutes. Add garlic and cook 1 minute longer. With a slotted spoon, transfer this mixture to the tart shell and distribute it over the cheese.

3 In a large bowl, whisk eggs and cream until blended. Mix in tomatoes, oregano, salt, and pepper and pour into the tart shell. Dot with remaining cheese. Bake in preheated 350°F oven about 40 minutes. Let rest for 10 minutes before serving.

Opposite: Mushrooms à la Carte (page 114).

Swiss Chard, Zucchini, and Ricotta Tart

SERVES 6 TO 8

This combination is one of the best in the book. It is a full meal, and delicious served with uncooked fresh tomato sauce. The lattice decoration is an extra step or two, but well worth it.

1 pound 6 ounces fresh Swiss chard or
    two 10-ounce packages frozen (to
    make 2 cups finely chopped leaves
    and stems, squeezed dry)
2 tablespoons vegetable or olive oil
2 tablespoons butter
1 cup finely chopped onion
1 garlic clove, finely chopped
4 large or 5 small eggs
1 cup whole or skim milk ricotta
1/4 cup finely chopped fresh parsley
1 cup freshly grated Parmesan or
    pecorino Romano cheese

1/2 cup light cream
salt
freshly ground pepper
pinch of freshly grated nutmeg
1 baked 8 × 11-inch tart shell, plus
    pastry for lattice strips (page 267)
1 small zucchini (1 × 6 inches), ends
    trimmed, cut into 1/8-inch slices
Uncooked Fresh Tomato Sauce
    (page 259)

1 If using fresh Swiss chard, wash and cook in boiling salted water. Drain and squeeze dry. If using frozen, cook, drain, and squeeze dry.

2 In a skillet, heat oil and butter and cook onion slowly until it colors. Add cooked Swiss chard and garlic and cook for several minutes to further dry out chard and to combine with onion. Transfer to a bowl and allow to cool.

3 Whisk eggs in large bowl. Add ricotta, parsley, 3/4 cup cheese, cream, salt, pepper, and nutmeg and mix well. Add cooled Swiss chard mixture and pour into baked shell. Bake in preheated 350°F oven for about 40 minutes, or until set.

4 As soon as tart is put into oven, place zucchini slices in boiling water, turn off heat, and let stand 10 minutes. Drain zucchini and pat dry.

5 When tart has baked 20 minutes, remove from oven and arrange lattice pastry on top of tart. Place a zucchini slice in the center of each lattice opening (you may have some left over). Distribute remaining Parmesan cheese on top of zucchini slices. Return to oven to complete baking. Allow to rest for 10 minutes or so before cutting.

6 If top of tart has not browned properly, run under broiler for a minute or two.

7 Serve with fresh tomato sauce.

Jerusalem Artichokes Baked in a Pie

SERVES 8

This is a very unusual and tasty vegetable presentation. It can be made with pie pastry or with four to six layers of buttered phyllo, brought together to form a pom-pom on top.

1 Basic Pastry recipe (page 267)
1 pound Jerusalem artichokes
  (sunchokes)
juice of ½ lemon
2 tablespoons (¼ stick) butter
2 tablespoons all-purpose flour
1 cup chicken stock, heated
2 cups fresh or frozen peas (one
  10-ounce package frozen)

2 cups finely diced cooked chicken,
  turkey, or meat
1 cup shredded smoked mozzarella
  (shred on large holes of hand grater)
½ teaspoon chopped fresh dill
½ teaspoon finely chopped lemon zest
salt
freshly ground pepper
1 egg (for brushing pastry)

1 Prepare the pastry and reserve ⅓ for another use. Using ⅔ of remaining piece, roll out 1 large circle to fit bottom and sides of 8 × 4-inch springform pan; fit into pan. Roll remaining piece into circle for top crust. Keep any leftover pastry for decoration.

2 Scrub artichokes with a brush (skin will lighten, and there is no need to scrape it away). Cut away any blemished areas. Cover whole artichokes with cool water mixed with juice of ½ lemon. Let stand at least 30 minutes (overnight in refrigerator if you wish). Slice *thinly* when ready to assemble pie.

3 Melt butter in small saucepan. Add flour and whisk 2 minutes. Add heated broth and whisk until sauce boils and thickens.

4 In a large bowl, combine sauce with artichoke slices, peas, chicken, mozzarella, dill, lemon zest, and salt and pepper to taste. Mix well and pour into pastry-lined springform. Fold over dough and cover with top layer of pastry, sealing edges of top layer to sides with fork tines. Brush entire surface with beaten egg. Decorate with pastry scraps, cut out as you wish. Cut vents in top to allow steam to escape.

5 Bake in preheated 375°F oven for 1½ hours or until pastry is nicely browned. Test for doneness by inserting sharp knife into pie. It should be like inserting a knife into a cooked potato. If there is too much resistance, continue baking until done.

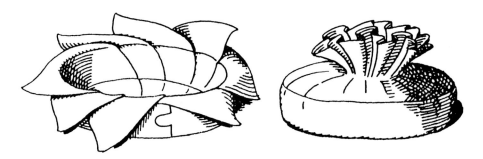

Butternut Squash with Curry Tart

SERVES 6 TO 8

6 tablespoons (¾ stick) butter
½ cup peeled apple slices
2 cups cooked, pureed butternut squash
1 cup finely chopped onion
¼ cup firmly packed brown sugar
¼ cup orange liqueur
1 tablespoon curry powder
3 eggs

½ cup light cream
salt
freshly ground pepper
1 baked 10-inch tart shell (page 267)
12 whole green onions, cleaned
½ cup Oil and Vinegar Dressing
  (page 261)

1 Melt 1 tablespoon butter in medium skillet. Add apple slices and sauté until tender. Puree apple in blender or food processor. Combine with squash in large bowl.

2 Melt 1 tablespoon butter in same skillet. Add onion and sauté until tender. Stir into squash mixture.

3 Melt remaining 4 tablespoons butter in same skillet. Add brown sugar, orange liqueur, and curry and cook until well blended and sugar is melted.

4 Add eggs, cream, salt, pepper, and curry mixture to squash and whisk until all is well blended. Taste and adjust seasoning. Pour into baked tart shell and bake in preheated 375°F oven for 50 to 60 minutes or until filling is set. Let rest for 10 or 15 minutes before serving.

5 Garnish each slice with 2 green onions. Spoon some dressing over the onion stalks.

Asparagus and Phyllo Tart

SERVES 8

See photo 3 following page 252.

24 asparagus stalks
1 cup low-fat yogurt
1 cup skim-milk ricotta
2 eggs, lightly beaten
1/4 cup finely chopped fresh parsley
1/2 cup finely chopped onion
1 teaspoon finely chopped orange zest

generous pinch of freshly grated nutmeg
salt and freshly ground pepper
7 sheets phyllo dough, about 11 × 16
  inches
4 tablespoons (1/2 stick) butter, melted
1/4 cup freshly grated Parmesan cheese

1 Snap off bottoms of asparagus stalks (remaining spears should be at least 4 inches long). Peel spears with a vegetable peeler and cook in boiling water until barely tender; do not overcook, as they will cook further in oven. Cut spears into 4-inch lengths, including tips. From leftover pieces cut enough thin slices to make 1 to 1½ cups. Set aside.

2 In a large bowl combine yogurt, ricotta, eggs, asparagus slices, parsley, onion, orange zest, nutmeg, and salt and pepper to taste. Mix well and set aside.

3 Brush phyllo with butter, one sheet at a time. Arrange sheets in 8 × 11-inch baking pan as follows: a. 2 buttered sheets across *length* of pan; b. 2 buttered sheets across *width* of pan; c. 2 buttered sheets across *length* of pan. Add filling, spreading evenly with rubber spatula. Fold over ends of phyllo to cover. Butter 7th phyllo sheet and fold in half crosswise. Lay on top of filled tart. Brush top with butter.

4 Sprinkle about half of Parmesan over the top sheet of phyllo. Bake in preheated 375°F oven for about 35 to 45 minutes, until filling is solid and top is golden. Remove from oven and lay asparagus spears side by side down one length of pan with flower ends pointing inward; repeat along other side, again with flower ends pointing inward. Sprinkle remaining Parmesan overall and return to oven for another 5 minutes. If top is not golden enough, run under broiler for a minute or so to brown pastry.

6

STUFFED VEGETABLES AND VEGETABLE STUFFINGS

Many vegetables make ideal shells for stuffing. Some require scooping out — eggplant, zucchini, peppers, and onions, for example — and others such as avocados and butternut squash have natural hollows ready for filling. Often the flesh which is removed may be used as part of the filling; onions, for instance, must be hollowed, but what is taken out may be chopped and added to the stuffing. Zucchini pulp may or may not be used for fillings, depending on the squash's maturity. The rule here is similar to that used for cucumbers: the pulp is not used if the seeds are large and fully developed.

On the other hand, in vegetable cookery the containers for stuffings need not be natural vegetable shells. Leaves make excellent wrappers: to mention just a few, collard greens, cabbage, lettuce, and Swiss chard, grape leaves, and corn husks.

The beauty of stuffing vegetables, and using them *as* stuffing, is not just in their taste but in the infinite variety of combinations, shapes, and colors that can be achieved. Stuffed vegetables can be baked, cooked on top of the stove, oven-broiled, and even charcoal-broiled.

Cold Artichokes with Bacon and Sour Cream Filling

SERVES 4

The artichokes can be cooked very early in the day, or the day before, and kept in the refrigerator. The sauce is delicious and the dish is fun to eat. See photo 4 following page 124.

4 artichokes
6 slices bacon
1 cup sour cream
3 tablespoons mayonnaise
2 tablespoons plus 1 teaspoon fresh
  lemon juice

3 tablespoons finely chopped fresh chives
salt
freshly ground pepper

1 Prepare artichokes for cooking (see page 14). Arrange them in a saucepan or flameproof casserole just large enough to hold them snugly in one layer. Add water to barely cover. Bring artichokes to a boil, lower heat and simmer half covered for about 40 minutes, or until tender (test for doneness by pulling off one or two outer leaves; if they come off easily, artichokes are done). Remove from hot water, drain, and refresh under cool water; turn upside down and drain well. Refrigerate artichokes.

2 While artichokes are cooking, fry bacon well, drain on paper towels and crumble.

3 Combine sour cream, mayonnaise, lemon juice, chives, salt, pepper, and bacon pieces. Mix well and taste for seasoning. Chill until shortly before serving time.

4 Turn artichokes top side up and open leaves as wide as possible. Remove chokes with a teaspoon. Fill center of each artichoke with bacon dressing and serve cold.

Stuffed Artichokes with a Light Aïoli Sauce

SERVES 6

Artichokes, one of the best natural food containers, can receive stuffings of all kinds. The following recipe calls for a spicy bread and sausage stuffing. Other fillings can be found on pages 103 and 108.

5 ounces sausage links, pepperoni,
   ham, or prosciutto
1 teaspoon olive oil
1½ cups fresh breadcrumbs
2 tablespoons chopped fresh parsley
2 garlic cloves, minced
3 eggs
¼ cup milk
6 tablespoons olive oil
salt
freshly ground pepper
6 large artichokes
½ cup fresh tomatoes, cored, blanched,
   peeled, seeded, and coarsely
   chopped, or canned plum tomatoes,
   drained and put through a food mill

12 small new potatoes
4 cups water
2 whole garlic cloves
4 carrots, each cut diagonally into
   3 pieces

AÏOLI SAUCE
(makes about 2 cups)
6 garlic cloves
2 small egg yolks
1 teaspoon fresh lemon juice
salt
white pepper
1 cup olive oil
½ cup light cream

1 Cut the meat into small pieces or slices. Heat 1 teaspoon olive oil in a small skillet and sauté the meat for about 5 minutes, stirring frequently. Drain the meat and transfer to a mixing bowl. Add the breadcrumbs, parsley, and minced garlic and toss well.

2 Beat eggs with milk and 2 tablespoons olive oil. Add to meat mixture. Add salt and pepper to taste and stir to blend.

3 Using a sharp knife, cut the stem off each artichoke to make a flat base. Pull off a few of the tough outer leaves. Cut off about ½ inch of the top of each artichoke and spread the leaves with your fingers. Invert the artichokes on a flat surface, pressing down on each one to open its leaves.

4 Divide filling into 6 equal parts. Turn each artichoke on its base and stuff the center first; then add filling between the leaves more or less at random, but be sure to push the stuffing down as you add it.

5 Select a flameproof casserole or Dutch oven just large enough to hold the artichokes snugly in one layer. If they do not fit close together in the casserole, tie each one around the center with string to help retain its shape. Arrange artichokes in the casserole, and spoon an equal amount of tomato on top of each. Add potatoes to the bottom of the casserole, fitting them in between the artichokes. Pour the water around them and add the whole garlic cloves to the water. Sprinkle the artichokes with the remaining 4 tablespoons olive oil. Cover the casserole and bring the liquid to a boil. Reduce heat and simmer until artichoke bottoms are tender, 45 minutes to 1 hour, adding carrot pieces after 20 minutes of cooking. To test for doneness, pull off an outside artichoke leaf; if it comes off easily, the artichokes are done.

6 While artichokes cook, prepare aïoli sauce: combine garlic, yolks, lemon juice, salt, and white pepper in food processor fitted with the metal blade. Process for a few seconds just to thoroughly combine. With motor running, *very slowly* pour oil in a fine stream down the feed tube; mixture will thicken. To thin somewhat, add half of the cream through the feed tube. Stop motor, scrape down sides and check for thickness — this sauce is meant to be *thinner* than mayonnaise. Blend in more light cream if necessary.

7 Remove artichokes and other vegetables from the casserole with a slotted spoon (do not serve the cooking liquid). Serve with light aïoli sauce, which is delicious with the potatoes, carrots, and artichokes.

Whole Savoy Cabbage with Four Stuffings

❦

SERVES 8

It is time to bring Savoy cabbage to the head of the vegetable parade, and this recipe does just that. The preparation sounds complex, but really isn't. It is delicious and a fantastic dish to present to company. See photo 2 following page 188.

1 large Savoy cabbage
4 cups fresh breadcrumbs
2 quarts chicken stock
4 eggs, beaten
8 tablespoons (1 stick) butter, melted
salt
freshly ground pepper
8 large parsley sprigs

BEET STUFFING
1 cup diced cooked beets
1 tablespoon chopped fresh chervil or
 1 teaspoon dried

RED PEPPER AND HAM
STUFFING
8 ounces cooked ham, diced
½ cup diced red bell pepper

CARROT STUFFING
1 cup diced cooked carrots
½ cup chopped onion, sautéed in
 1 tablespoon butter

CHESTNUT STUFFING
1 cup chopped cooked chestnuts
8 slices bacon, cooked until crisp,
 drained, and crumbled

MUSTARD SAUCE
(makes about 2 cups)
4 tablespoons (½ stick) butter
¼ cup all-purpose flour
2 cups chicken stock from cooking
 cabbage, heated
¼ cup Dijon mustard
salt
freshly ground pepper

1 Wash the cabbage and remove any blemishes, but leave outer leaves intact. Remove some of the core with a sharp knife, creating an opening large enough to hold some stuffing. Soak the cabbage in cold water for at least 1 hour or as long as overnight. Drain.

2 Bring salted water to a boil in a saucepan just a little larger than the head of cabbage. Blanch the cabbage for 10 minutes, 2 or 3 minutes longer if the head is very large (the object is to be able to separate the leaves from the core without breaking them). Drain upside down in a large colander. Let cool until cabbage can be handled.

3 Combine breadcrumbs, 1 cup chicken stock, eggs, butter, salt, and pepper and toss to mix well. Divide into 4 portions. To each portion add a group of ingredients listed above to make 4 separate stuffings.

4 Put cabbage core side up on a large platter of work surface. Fill core with some beet stuffing. Turn over and, one by one, spread out cabbage leaves until you reach the center of the cabbage; if the very 2 or 3 center leaves won't separate, don't fret. Continue with the beet stuffing, starting at the very center of the cabbage by stuffing the inside leaves. Reclose this layer of leaves. Working toward the outside of the cabbage, next use the red pepper and ham stuffing, then the carrot and chestnut stuffings, reforming the cabbage as you go.

5 Lay out 3 or 4 thicknesses of cheesecloth, each 2 feet square. Carefully move stuffed cabbage, core side down, to center of cloth. Tie opposite ends of cloth on top so cabbage is tightly enclosed. Return cabbage to the pan in which it was blanched and add remaining chicken stock to just cover the cabbage. Bring to a boil, lower heat, cover and simmer for 45 minutes or until cabbage is tender and done. Remove cabbage to drain, reserving liquid for sauce. Allow to drain well before removing cloth covering. Set cabbage on large serving platter and garnish with parsley sprigs. To serve, cut into wedges, place on individual plates, and spoon sauce alongside; do not pour sauce on top. Each cabbage wedge will show the deep reds, pinks, and oranges of the various vegetable stuffings.

6 For sauce, melt butter in a saucepan and allow it to bubble. Add flour and whisk constantly for 2 minutes. Add heated stock and whisk until sauce boils and thickens. Remove from heat, add mustard, and mix well. Thin with additional stock or cream if thinner sauce is desired. Season with salt and pepper.

NOTE

For presentation, slices of cooked beets, carrots, and raw red pepper may be arranged around cabbage and served with sauce.

❧

Artichokes Stuffed with a Little Lamb

SERVES 6

2 tablespoons vegetable, corn, or olive oil
1½ cups finely chopped green onions,
  shallots, or onions
2 garlic cloves, finely chopped
8 ounces mushrooms, chopped
12 ounces lean ground lamb
3 tablespoons chopped fresh dill or
  1 teaspoon dried dillweed

3 tablespoons chopped fresh parsley
1 tablespoon finely chopped lemon zest
½ cup toasted pine nuts
salt
freshly ground pepper
6 large artichokes prepared for stuffing
  (see page 104, step 3)

1 Heat oil in skillet and sauté onions just until transparent. Add garlic and mushrooms and sauté 5 minutes. Remove from heat.

2 In a large bowl combine lamb, dill, parsley, lemon zest, pine nuts, and the onion/mushroom mixture. Mix well and season to taste with salt and pepper. Divide into 6 portions and stuff each artichoke (see page 105, step 4).

3 Arrange artichokes in flameproof casserole or Dutch oven just large enough to hold them snugly in one layer. Pour water into casserole (not over artichokes) to come midway up artichokes. Cover and bring to boil. Reduce heat and simmer 45 minutes to 1 hour, until artichokes are tender. Remove with slotted spoon and serve hot.

Opposite: Gougère with Tomato and Cumin
(page 244).

Stuffed Christophenes

SERVES 6

This tropical squash, also called *chayote* or vegetable pear, is available in Latin American and specialty food shops.

3 chayotes, about 12 ounces each
1/3 cup butter
1 medium onion, minced
celery salt
seasoned salt

freshly ground pepper
1 cup shredded Cheddar cheese
1/2 cup plus 2 tablespoons fine dry
   breadcrumbs
freshly grated Parmesan cheese

1 Bring enough salted water to cover chayotes to boil over medium high heat. Add whole squashes and cook until almost tender, about 30 minutes. Drain and cool.

2 Preheat oven to 350°F. Cut the chayotes in half lengthwise. Scoop pulp, including the edible seeds, into a medium bowl; set shells aside. Add butter and onion to pulp with celery salt and seasoned salt to taste and mash well. Taste for seasoning. Fold in Cheddar cheese and 1/2 cup breadcrumbs. Fill shells evenly. Top with remaining crumbs and sprinkle with Parmesan. Bake 15 minutes or until lightly brown. Serve warm.

Opposite: Risotto Primavera (page 149).

Vegetable and Pork Filling in Phyllo

❦

SERVES 10

Oriental flavors packed in Greek pastry—both are now part of the American scene. This is a very savory dish; add a little salad and you'll have a wonderful meal. See photo 1 opposite page 60.

2 cups broccoli flowerets
2 tablespoons soy sauce
¼ cup water
1½ teaspoons cornstarch
1 teaspoon sugar
3 tablespoons peanut oil
2 center-cut pork chops, trimmed of fat
   and cut into ¼-inch cubes (about
   1 cup)

2 large garlic cloves, finely chopped
1 teaspoon grated fresh ginger
1 large red bell pepper, cored, seeded,
   and cut into 1-inch squares
2 tablespoons toasted sesame seed
15 sheets phyllo dough (see note)
1½ cups (3 sticks) unsalted butter,
   melted

1 Drop broccoli into boiling water and cook 3 minutes. Drain and set aside.

2 In a small bowl combine soy sauce, water, cornstarch, and sugar. Mix well and set aside.

3 Heat oil in a large saucepan over moderately high heat. Add pork and stir fry 2 minutes. Add garlic and ginger and stir fry 1 minute; add red pepper and stir fry 2 minutes. Add the broccoli flowerets and the soy sauce mixture and stir well for 1 minute. Remove from heat.

4 Coat the bottom of a small saucepan very lightly with peanut oil. Add sesame seed and toast over medium heat until lightly browned, about 1 to 2 minutes. Add to vegetable mixture.

5 Cut phyllo sheets in half lengthwise (you will have 30 half sheets). Brush one sheet with melted butter. Place another sheet on top and brush with butter. Add one more sheet to make a stack of 3 layers. Place about

1 tablespoon of filling mixture at one end of the layered phyllo sheets and fold over at an angle to begin forming a triangle. Continue to fold at an angle, brushing each surface with butter, until you reach the end of the phyllo. Trim off any excess dough. Repeat with remaining phyllo and filling. Arrange the triangles seam side down on a large baking sheet. Bake in preheated 400°F oven for 10 to 15 minutes, or until golden brown. Serve hot, accompanied by hot pepper jelly.

NOTE

Try to purchase fresh phyllo, available in gourmet and food specialty shops. It's much easier to work with than frozen sheets of dough, and will not tear as easily. Use what you need, then wrap the remaining phyllo in its own wrapper and more plastic wrap. It will keep in the refrigerator for 3 to 4 weeks; do not freeze.

Three Stuffed Vegetables: Red Bell Peppers, Eggplants, and Tomatoes

SERVES 6 TO 8

This is adapted from Tess Mallos' *Yemista* preparation. Choose medium-size vegetables and use Italian- or Japanese-type eggplants; they are small and long.

6 red bell peppers
6 Italian or Japanese eggplants
6 medium tomatoes
½ cup (or more) vegetable oil
2 onions, finely chopped
1½ pounds lean ground lamb
3 garlic cloves, finely chopped
1 cup raw long-grain rice

3 tablespoons chopped fresh mint or
   1 teaspoon dried
2 tablespoons chopped fresh parsley
3 tablespoons sugar
salt
freshly ground pepper
½ cup beef stock
2-inch cinnamon stick

1 Slice tops off peppers to create a large enough opening to stuff peppers easily. Reserve tops. Cut out membranes and remove seeds from peppers. Wash peppers and tops, dry, and set aside. Lay the eggplants on their sides and cut lengthwise making the cut ¼th deep; reserve this. Scoop out the pulp from the larger pieces, creating "boats" approximately ¼ inch thick. Put eggplants, including reserved tops and portion scooped out, in salted water for 20 minutes. Drain, rinse, and dry. Wash tomatoes and slice ¼ to ½ inch off tops. Remove pulp and put through food mill; reserve.

2 In large skillet or saucepan (with cover) heat 2 tablespoons oil and cook onion until it just begins to color, about 5 minutes. Add lamb and break it up with a wooden spoon. Increase heat and cook until lamb is no longer red; do not overcook. Add garlic, ½ cup tomato puree, rice, mint, parsley, 2 tablespoons sugar, salt, and pepper. Lower heat, cover, and simmer 15 minutes, or until most of liquid is absorbed. Sauté eggplant pulp in 1 tablespoon oil in another skillet. Add to lamb mixture. Taste and adjust seasoning. Stuff all the vegetables, remembering that the filling will expand as it cooks. Heat 1 tablespoon oil and sauté eggplant tops, using more oil if needed. Replace vegetable tops and arrange close together in oven-proof dish.

3 Combine ¼ cup oil, remaining tomato puree, beef stock, cinnamon stick, 1 tablespoon sugar, and salt and pepper to taste in a bowl. Pour over vegetables and cover with foil. Bake in preheated 350°F oven for 1 hour. Remove foil, baste vegetables with sauce, and continue baking for 30 minutes longer or until all vegetables are tender.

VARIATION

In filling, use 1½ pounds ground lamb, ½ cup bulgur, ¼ cup rice, and a pinch of red pepper flakes. Follow all other directions.

Mushrooms à la carte

An appetizing way to serve mushrooms is to stuff them with a variety of fillings; make all three for a hearty meal. Select mushrooms of equal size, about 2 to 2½ inches in diameter. A sliced cucumber and radish salad is a good accompaniment. See photo 2 following page 92.

Mushrooms with Garlic Butter and Parsley

MAKES 12

12 large mushrooms
2 tablespoons finely chopped lemon zest
2 tablespoons strained fresh lemon juice
salt
freshly ground pepper

2 tablespoons butter
2 garlic cloves, finely chopped
½ cup finely chopped fresh parsley, preferably flat-leaf
6 tablespoons fresh breadcrumbs

1 Carefully remove the stem from each mushroom; if part of stem is still attached to cap, cut it away with a small paring knife. Reserve stems for another use. Wipe each mushroom cap with a damp towel; do not wash.

2 Preheat oven to 375°F. Arrange the mushrooms on a tray and add the lemon zest and lemon juice to concave bottom of each cap. Season with salt and pepper.

3 Melt butter in a skillet over medium-high heat, add the garlic, and sauté 1 to 2 minutes; be sure garlic does not brown. Remove from heat and add parsley, breadcrumbs, salt, and pepper and toss well.

4 Fill each cap with the mixture. Bake for 15 minutes, watching carefully for the last few minutes of baking; the mushroom caps should stay firm, not fall apart.

Mushrooms with Hazelnuts and Butter

MAKES 12

12 large mushrooms
2 tablespoons strained fresh lemon juice
salt
freshly ground pepper
4 tablespoons (½ stick) unsalted butter
½ cup finely chopped hazelnuts
¼ cup fresh breadcrumbs

1 Prepare mushrooms according to instructions in step 1 of previous recipe. Lay the mushroom caps on a tray and sprinkle with lemon juice. Season with salt and pepper.

2 Preheat oven to 375°F. Melt butter in a skillet over medium-high heat, add hazelnuts, and sauté for 1 minute, stirring constantly. Remove from heat.

3 Fill each mushroom cap with the hazelnut and butter mixture. Sprinkle with breadcrumbs. Bake 15 minutes, or until golden brown, watching carefully for the last few minutes of baking; the mushroom caps should stay firm, not fall apart.

Mushrooms with Spinach

MAKES 12

12 large mushrooms
4 tablespoons (½ stick) unsalted butter
2 shallots, finely chopped
1 cup cooked, chopped fresh spinach, well drained, or one 10-ounce package frozen spinach, cooked, drained, and finely chopped

2 tablespoons crème fraîche or whipping cream
salt
freshly ground pepper

115

1 Prepare mushrooms according to instruction in step 1 of recipe for Mushrooms with Garlic Butter and Parsley (page 114). Melt 2 tablespoons butter in skillet over medium-high heat. Add shallots and sauté for 1 to 2 minutes; do not let shallots brown. Add the spinach and toss well until heated through. Add crème fraîche or cream. Season with salt and pepper and mix well.

2 Preheat oven to 375°F. Arrange mushrooms on a tray, salt and pepper each cap, and fill caps with spinach mixture, mounding it slightly. Cut remaining 2 tablespoons butter into 12 pieces and top each cap with a piece of butter. Bake for 15 minutes or until golden brown.

Peppers with Leeks, Cheese, and Eggs

SERVES 3

6 unblemished long orange or yellow
  sweet peppers
salt
¼ cup vegetable oil
1 cup chopped leeks
1 garlic clove, finely chopped
2 large eggs, beaten

2 tablespoons chopped fresh flat-leaf
  parsley
1 tablespoon chopped fresh basil or
  1 teaspoon dried
1 cup shredded sharp white Cheddar
  cheese

1 Cut off the stem end of each pepper; reserve. Halve peppers lengthwise to about 1½ inches from narrow end; do not cut all the way through peppers. Remove seeds carefully, being careful not to break or split the peppers. Salt each pepper and set aside. Finely chop removed tops of peppers, along with enough flesh trimmed from opened ends, to make 1 cup.

2 Heat oil in a large skillet. Add the chopped pepper and sauté for 3 minutes. Add leeks and sauté for 2 minutes more. Add garlic and sauté an additional 1 minute. Season with salt and pepper and mix well.

3 Preheat oven to 375°F. Fill each pepper half with the mixture and place in oiled baking pan or casserole big enough to hold the peppers in one layer. Cover loosely with foil and bake peppers for 25 to 30 minutes.

4 In a bowl mix eggs, parsley, basil, Cheddar cheese, salt, and pepper and beat well. Carefully spoon the egg mixture on top of each pepper and bake an additional 10 minutes or until browned. If the pepper stuffing is not brown enough, set peppers under the broiler for 1 to 2 minutes. Serve hot.

Cauliflower and Carrots with Turkey in Pastry

SERVES 6

The "pie crust" here is multiple sheets of phyllo pastry, baked in a springform pan with layers of vegetables and some turkey.

3 tablespoons unsalted butter
2 large onions, finely chopped (about 2 cups)
3 large carrots, finely chopped (about 1 cup)
2 garlic cloves, finely chopped
1 teaspoon dried chervil
½ cup crème fraîche
1½ tablespoons fresh lemon juice
1½ teaspoons Dijon mustard

2 cups cooked turkey breast cut into 1-inch cubes
salt
freshly ground pepper
1 medium cauliflower
2 cups grated Gruyère cheese about 4 ounces
2 eggs, beaten
12 ounces (about) phyllo dough (see note)
1 cup (2 sticks) unsalted butter, melted

1 Melt 3 tablespoons butter in large saucepan and sauté onions for 2 minutes. Add the carrots, garlic, and chervil and cook 2 minutes.

2 In a bowl combine the cooked vegetables, crème fraîche, lemon juice, mustard, turkey, salt, and pepper. Mix well and taste for seasoning.

3 Cut the cauliflower head in half and remove the core. Cut cauliflower into flowerets and cook them in boiling salted water for 2 to 3 minutes; do not overcook. Drain well.

4 In a medium bowl combine the cauliflower, cheese, eggs, salt, and pepper. Mix well.

5 Set rack in middle of oven and preheat oven to 375°F. Line the bottom of a buttered 9-inch springform pan with 1 folded sheet of phyllo dough. Brush the sheet with melted butter. Continue to layer 8 more buttered sheets. Spoon in ⅓ of the cauliflower mixture and ⅓ of the turkey mixture. Fold the overhanging dough over the turkey. Layer 4 more buttered

phyllo sheets; spoon in ⅓ of the cauliflower mixture and ⅓ of the turkey mixture. Do not fold the overhanging dough yet; continue with 4 more buttered sheets of dough, spoon in remaining cauliflower and turkey mixtures, and finish with 4 sheets of buttered phyllo. Fold the overhanging dough around the rim of the pan to make a high edge. Brush the surface with butter. Cut a few slits in the top.

6 Bake for 50 to 55 minutes, or until top of pastry is golden. Let stand for 10 to 15 minutes, then loosen the edge with a knife before removing the springform.

NOTE

Try to purchase fresh phyllo, available in gourmet and food specialty shops. It's much easier to work with than frozen sheets of dough, and will not tear as easily. Use what you need, then wrap the remaining phyllo in its own wrapper and more plastic wrap. It will keep in the refrigerator for 3 to 4 weeks; do not freeze.

Zucchini Baskets

SERVES 4 TO 6

This dish is so good it makes the whole book worthwhile. It is easy to prepare—given a little patience in cutting the zucchini—and the taste is extraordinary. Serve two baskets per person as a main dish (some will want more), or serve one per person as an appetizer.

12 uniform-size medium zucchini, (about 1½ × 6 inches), cooked in boiling salted water until tender (do not overcook) and drained
2 tablespoons butter
1 cup finely chopped green onions (including tender green parts)
6 fresh basil leaves, finely chopped or 1 teaspoon dried
6 fresh mint leaves, finely chopped or 1 teaspoon dried

¾ to 1 cup peeled, seeded, and finely chopped fresh tomatoes (or equivalent in canned plum tomatoes, but try to use fresh)
salt
freshly ground pepper
1 cup fresh or frozen green peas (if fresh, cook until crisp-tender; if frozen, thaw)
1 cup Mornay Sauce (page 256)
6 slices bacon, cut in half crosswise

1 Trim ends from zucchini and lay each one flat (if a zucchini won't lay flat, cut a very thin slice from one side to allow it to sit firmly; usually this is not necessary). With a small sharp knife make 2 shallow crosswise cuts about ¾ inch apart in the center top of each zucchini (these will make the basket handle). Slice down in one of the cuts halfway through the zucchini. Go to that end of the zucchini and cut through horizontally to the center, cutting away approximately ¼ of the whole vegetable except for the handle part. Repeat on the other end. With a small melon baller or spoon scrape away pulp in entire bottom half. Cut away under basket handle. Peel off green skin of cut-away parts, chop finely, and set aside. Discard zucchini pulp.

2 Melt butter in skillet and sauté onions until transparent. Add chopped zucchini skin, basil, mint, tomatoes, salt, and pepper and simmer for 3 minutes. Add peas and Mornay Sauce, mix well and remove from heat. Taste and adjust seasoning. Carefully fill baskets. Arrange in baking pan or casserole which will contain zucchini baskets snugly.

3 Coil raw bacon slices to simulate a rose and pierce bottom with a toothpick. Place bacon rose on top of zucchini basket at one side of handle, piercing toothpick into filling. Bake baskets in preheated 350°F oven for 30 minutes. Serve hot and crisp.

Mrs. Burson's Lettuce Packages

SERVES 4

The Bursons of Birmingham, Alabama, bring life to these lettuce leaves.

12 ounces ground pork
1 egg
1/4 cup cornstarch
2 tablespoons soy sauce
1/2 cup corn oil
1/2 cup finely diced bamboo shoots
12 water chestnuts, finely diced
6 to 8 dried (porcini) mushrooms,
    soaked for 10 minutes in hot water,
    stems cut off

1 1/2 teaspoons sugar
2 tablespoons dry Sherry
1 tablespoon water
1 cup finely diced celery
salt
lettuce leaves

1 Mix pork, egg, 2 tablespoons cornstarch, and soy sauce and let stand for 15 minutes.

2 Gently heat oil in large skillet. Add pork and stir until pieces separate.

3 Stir in bamboo shoots, water chestnuts, and mushrooms.

4 Add sugar and stir fry 2 minutes. Stir in Sherry.

5 Combine remaining 2 tablespoons cornstarch with water and add to skillet a little at a time just until mixture begins to thicken. Stir in celery and season with salt if necessary.

6 Serve with lettuce leaves. Place a dab of filling on each leaf and fold leaf over into a package. If you wish, the packages can be tied with, for example, a string of celery.

Stuffed Tomatoes

We could do a book on stuffing tomatoes, and if we were to cull five favorite recipes from it these would be the ones. The first preparation is very elegant—tomato aspic-filled tomatoes topped with caviar and accompanied by a creamy sauce. The other recipes all have their own distinctive flavors, such as curry, raisins and nuts, or parsley, bread, and onion.

❦

Tomato Aspic in Fresh Tomatoes with Caviar

SERVES 8

8 medium tomatoes
salt
½ cup caviar
8 radishes, cut into flowers
8 fresh mint sprigs
8 radicchio leaves
Horseradish Cream Sauce (page 264)

ASPIC
3 cups (about) coarsely chopped fresh tomatoes (or fresh tomatoes and canned plum tomatoes, including liquid)

1 small onion, coarsely chopped
4 celery stalks with leaves, coarsely chopped
2 tablespoons chopped fresh mint or 1 teaspoon dried
2 tablespoons fresh lemon juice
1 tablespoon sugar
1 teaspoon salt
1 bay leaf
2 packets (¼ ounce each) unflavored gelatin
½ cup cool water

1 Wash and core the tomatoes. Blanch for 30 seconds, and remove the skins, being sure not to puncture the tomatoes in the process. Widen the opening of each tomato by cutting away more at the stem end. Scoop the pulp from the tomatoes and place in a measuring cup; add the pieces which were cut away in widening the core openings. Salt the inside of each tomato and turn it over to drain for 30 minutes.

2 To make the aspic, add enough fresh or canned tomatoes to the reserved pulp and tomato pieces to make 3½ cups. Combine the tomatoes, onion, celery, mint, lemon juice, sugar, salt, and bay leaf in a large saucepan. Bring to boil and simmer for 30 minutes.

3 Strain mixture through several layers of cheesecloth; discard the pulp. (You should have 3 cups hot tomato liquid.) Soften gelatin in the cool water and add to the hot tomato liquid, stirring well to dissolve gelatin completely. Pour aspic mixture into a glass or ceramic bowl and refrigerate until almost set.

4 Turn the empty tomato shells right side up and pat them dry, inside and out. When the aspic is almost set, spoon some of it into each shell, piling it as high in the tomato as you can. Carefully spoon 1 tablespoon caviar on top of each tomato. Garnish with a radish and a mint sprig and place each tomato on a radicchio leaf. Serve with Horseradish Cream Sauce.

Opposite: Vegetable Bundles Vinaigrette (page 166).
Following page: Okra and Cornmeal Pudding with
Old-Fashioned Spicy Tomato Sauce (page 160).

Stuffed Tomatoes with Basil, Eggs, and Breadcrumbs

SERVES 2 TO 4

4 medium to large tomatoes
salt
3 slices bread
2 hard-cooked eggs
1 whole egg, lightly beaten

1 tablespoon oil
2 tablespoons chopped fresh basil or
* 1 teaspoon dried*
freshly ground pepper
1 tablespoon butter

1 Wash and core tomatoes. Widen the opening of each tomato by cutting away more at the stem end. Chop tomato pulp into small bits, drain well, and place in a mixing bowl.

2 Salt the inside of each tomato, turn upside down, and allow to drain for 30 minutes.

3 Remove crust from bread, cut bread into pieces, and grind to crumbs in food processor (you should have 1 cup). Add to drained tomato pulp. Chop eggs coarsely and add to tomato with beaten egg, oil, basil, and pepper; mix well. Taste and adjust seasoning.

4 Fill each tomato with stuffing. Arrange in a baking dish, dot with butter, and bake in preheated 350°F oven for 30 to 40 minutes, depending on size of tomatoes, or until done.

Opposite: Cold Artichokes with Bacon and
Sour Cream Filling (page 103).
Preceding page: Pizza with Vegetable Topping
(page 242).

Stuffed Tomatoes with Mint, Parsley, Raisins, Nuts, and Rice

SERVES 6

12 large, firm tomatoes (not overripe)
1 teaspoon salt
½ cup olive oil
1 cup finely chopped onion
1 cup grated or shredded carrot
1 cup raw long-grain rice
½ cup pine nuts

½ cup raisins
1½ cups chicken stock or vegetable broth
⅓ cup finely chopped fresh mint or
   2 teaspoons dried
½ cup finely chopped fresh parsley
2 tablespoons sugar
½ cup dry white wine

1 Wash and dry the tomatoes; remove stems, if any. Slice off the top of each tomato and reserve. Carefully scoop out the pulp from each tomato and transfer to a bowl. Lightly salt insides of tomatoes and turn them upside down to drain for 30 minutes.

2 Meanwhile, heat 2 tablespoons olive oil in a large skillet and sauté onion until it begins to color. Add carrot and rice and cook for 2 to 3 minutes, stirring frequently.

3 Add pine nuts, raisins, stock or broth, mint, ¼ cup parsley, and sugar. Bring to boil, lower heat, cover, and cook for 10 minutes; most of the liquid should be absorbed by the rice. Remove from heat.

4 Stuff the tomatoes with rice mixture and arrange them in a baking dish just large enough to hold them snugly.

5 Process tomato pulp through a food mill. Salt and pepper to taste and add to the baking dish, but not over the tomatoes. Add the wine to the baking dish also. Sprinkle remaining olive oil into the filled tomatoes, recap and bake in preheated 350°F oven for 30 minutes. Sprinkle remaining parsley atop tomato caps before serving hot or cold.

Stuffed Tomatoes with Chicken, Peas, and Potatoes

SERVES 4

One of these stuffed tomatoes makes a meal, especially if you serve it with cooked green beans and thin slices of cooked carrot. Marinate these extra vegetables in some of the vinaigrette sauce. See photo 2 following page 252.

4 medium to large tomatoes
salt
1 cup cooked potatoes cut into ½-inch
 cubes
½ cup cooked fresh or frozen green peas
1 cup cooked white chicken meat cut
 into ½-inch cubes
1 tablespoon chopped fresh tarragon or
 1 teaspoon dried

2 tablespoons capers
4 anchovy filets, chopped fine
freshly ground pepper
1 cup Oil and Vinegar Dressing
 (page 261)
4 large or 8 small radicchio leaves
4 green onions, thinly sliced lengthwise

1 Wash and core tomatoes. Widen the opening of each tomato by cutting away more at the stem end. Carefully scoop out the pulp from each tomato, chop coarsely, and transfer to mixing bowl. Salt the inside of each tomato, turn upside down, and allow to drain for 30 minutes.

2 Add potatoes, peas, chicken, tarragon, capers, anchovy and pepper to tomato pulp. Add ½ cup dressing and toss well. Add more dressing if mixture seems dry. Taste and adjust seasoning.

3 Arrange radicchio leaves on individual plates or one large serving platter. Place tomatoes on top and stuff them generously. Scatter green onion slivers alongside tomatoes. Spoon a bit of additional dressing over all; pass any remaining dressing separately.

Tomatoes Stuffed with Rice and Curry

SERVES 6

6 large, firm-ripe tomatoes
salt
1½ cups chicken stock or vegetable broth
½ cup raw long-grain rice
4 tablespoons (½ stick) unsalted butter
1 medium onion, finely chopped
1 medium-size tart apple, peeled and
　coarsely chopped

1 teaspoon white wine vinegar
2 tablespoons curry powder
¼ cup raisins
salt
freshly ground pepper

1 Cut a thin slice from the top of each tomato and scoop out most of the pulp, leaving the walls of the tomato thick enough to hold a filling. Salt the inside of each tomato, invert on a rack, and drain for 20 minutes.

2 Bring the stock or broth to a rapid boil, add the rice, lower the heat, cover, and simmer for 15 minutes or until rice is done.

3 Preheat oven to 400°F. Melt the butter in skillet over medium heat, add onion, and cook for 3 minutes. Add apple and cook 3 minutes more. Stir in the vinegar and curry powder. Remove from heat and add the rice, raisins, salt if needed, and pepper. Toss well. Taste and adjust seasoning.

4 Fill the tomatoes lightly with the rice mixture, mounding it slightly. Arrange the tomatoes in a lightly oiled pan, cover with foil, and bake for 15 minutes; do not overcook (tomatoes should hold their shape and be firm but tender). Serve hot.

7

ROULADES, CREPES, AND OTHER VEGETABLE ROLLS

Vegetables create a cornucopia of imaginative meals which come in almost any shape, size, or design. This chapter gives us more opportunities to create vegetable entrees for brunch, lunch, supper, or buffet table by preparing vegetable rolls.

Soufflé rolls or roulades can themselves be made with vegetables and then receive a vegetable filling. When presented, there is nothing more attractive; when eaten, nothing tastier. Simple-to-make crepes roll easily and are ideal for zesty vegetable fillings.

Of course, many vegetables themselves offer the ultimate rolled container: Swiss chard, cabbage leaves, and eggplant slices are just a few examples. Since there has never been a more exciting time in American culinary history, try these and create some of your own fresh and richly rewarding recipes.

Crepes Filled with a Spinach and Cheese Soufflé

MAKES 8 FILLED CREPES

The spinach and cheese soufflé mixture is added to a flat crepe, baked, and then rolled lightly. See photo 2 following page 220.

¼ cup cold milk
3 tablespoons all-purpose flour
¾ cup milk
generous pinch of freshly grated nutmeg
salt
freshly ground pepper
4 egg yolks

½ cup freshly grated Parmesan cheese
1 tablespoon butter
1 cup cooked, drained, and chopped spinach
5 egg whites
8 crepes (page 268)
Sauce Bâtarde (page 255)

1 Combine ¼ cup cold milk and flour; set aside. In a saucepan, scald ¾ cup milk, blend in the flour mixture and cook this until thickened. Add the nutmeg and salt and pepper to taste. Remove from heat and allow the mixture to cool for 4 to 5 minutes. Blend in egg yolks one at a time. Add the cheese and blend well. Set the mixture aside.

2 Melt the butter in a small pan. Add the spinach and heat through. Blend the heated spinach into the cheese mixture.

3 Whip the egg whites until they form stiff peaks. Fold about ⅓ of the egg whites into the spinach mixture, then fold in the remaining whites.

4 Place the 8 crepes flat on 1 or 2 buttered baking sheets. Spoon equal amounts of the soufflé mixture onto the center of the crepes. Bake in preheated 400°F oven until the soufflé is puffy and browned. Roll the crepes and serve them immediately with Sauce Bâtarde.

131

Zucchini Roulade with Swiss Chard Filling

SERVES 8

In summer this is particularly good served with sliced ripe tomatoes.

1¼ pounds zucchini
1 teaspoon salt
4 tablespoons (½ stick) unsalted butter
¼ cup vegetable oil
½ cup finely chopped onion
⅓ cup all-purpose flour
1 cup milk, heated
4 eggs, separated
½ cup grated pecorino Romano cheese
½ cup very fine breadcrumbs

FILLING
3 tablespoons vegetable oil
2 onions, finely chopped
1 garlic clove, finely chopped
2 cups chopped cooked Swiss chard or
  spinach
½ cup grated pecorino Romano cheese

1 Wash the zucchini in cool water, dry them and trim both ends. Shred on large holes of grater (or with shredding blade of food processor) and put in a colander or large strainer. Sprinkle with salt, toss, and allow to drain for 20 to 30 minutes. Squeeze out as much moisture as possible. Set aside.

2 Heat butter and oil in a saucepan and sauté the onion until it is wilted and just begins to color. Mix in the flour and cook 3 minutes, stirring constantly (the flour should begin to color).

3 Pour in milk and whisk until mixture boils and is thick and smooth. Remove from heat and cool for 10 minutes. Whisk in egg yolks and ½ cup cheese, then fold in zucchini. Whip egg whites until stiff. Fold half of egg whites into zucchini mixture, then fold in remaining whites. Taste and adjust seasoning.

4 Lightly butter or oil a 10 × 15-inch jelly roll pan. Sprinkle breadcrumbs overall (tap pan at an angle on countertop to spread evenly, then shake out excess crumbs). With a spatula, spread zucchini mixture as evenly as you can make it. Tap bottom of pan lightly on work surface. Bake in preheated 375°F oven for 15 to 20 minutes, or until roulade is puffed and leaves sides of pan. Allow to cool for a few minutes. Run knife around edges to loosen, then turn roulade out onto kitchen towel. Do not turn off oven.

5 Meanwhile, for filling, heat oil in a skillet, add onions and garlic, and sauté for 2 minutes; do not let onions or garlic brown.

6 Add onions and garlic to Swiss chard. Add ½ cup cheese and mix thoroughly.

7 Spread filling over roulade and roll up jelly roll style, using towel as aid. Keep roll as tight as you can. Place seam side down on jelly roll pan and return to oven for 5 minutes to heat through, then run roulade under broiler for 2 minutes or until golden brown. Serve immediately.

Carrot Cannelloni with Vegetables

❧

SERVES 6 TO 8 (MAKES 25)

Stuffed pastas need not always be filled with meat. In this cannelloni dish the pasta itself is made with a vegetable puree; then it is filled with three or four other vegetables and sauced. See photo 1 opposite page 252.

CARROT PASTA
2½ cups all-purpose flour
1 egg
1 tablespoon olive oil
1 teaspoon salt
2 carrots, sliced, cooked, and pureed
   (⅔ cup)
5 tablespoons warm water

FILLING
4 tablespoons (½ stick) unsalted butter
1 whole boned, skinned chicken breast
1 medium onion, finely chopped
   (about ½ cup)

2 garlic cloves, finely chopped
2 tablespoons dry Marsala
1 cup thinly sliced mushrooms
8 ounces cooked spinach, drained and
   coarsely chopped (about 2 cups)
1 cup ricotta
1 tablespoon finely chopped fresh
   tarragon or 1 teaspoon dried
¼ cup freshly grated Parmesan cheese
salt
freshly ground pepper
2 cups Bechamel Sauce (page 255)

1 Make the pasta first. Place 2 cups flour in a medium bowl. Make a well in the center and add the egg, olive oil, salt, pureed carrots, and water. Mix well to form a dough.

2 Transfer dough to a floured board and knead for about 15 minutes or until smooth, gradually adding reserved flour as needed. Form the dough into a ball, cover it with a bowl, and let it rest for 15 minutes.

3 Roll the dough into a cylinder 6 to 7 inches long, then slice it into ½-inch pieces. Flatten the pieces of dough slightly with a rolling pin or the palm of your hand.

4 Using a hand crank pasta machine, run each ball of dough through the rollers' largest opening two times without folding. Gradually decrease size of opening and pass each dough piece through. It is not necessary to put dough through each setting. You can skip every other one — for example, on a 6-setting machine, roll dough through openings 6 (the thickest), 4, 2, and 1 (the thinnest). Very lightly flour each strip of dough after it is rolled out. Run the palm of your hand up and down the strip to coat it evenly with flour.

5 For cannelloni, cut the pasta into 3 × 4-inch rectangles; you will need 25. There will be some pasta left over; dry and freeze in bags for another use. Pasta can be made early in the day; arrange cut cannelloni on clean kitchen towels (do not stack or they will stick together). Cover and set aside.

6 For filling, melt 2 tablespoons butter in saucepan and sauté the chicken breast until lightly browned. Remove chicken and set aside. In the same saucepan sauté onion and garlic for 1 minute. Add Marsala and mushrooms and sauté for 2 minutes more.

7 Cut the chicken into several pieces and chop finely in food processor. Transfer to large bowl and add mushroom mixture, spinach, ricotta, tarragon, Parmesan cheese, salt, and pepper. Mix well and taste for seasoning.

8 Preheat oven to 375°F. Spoon 1 very large tablespoon of the spinach mixture onto each pasta square. Roll up tightly. Butter a baking dish large enough to hold 25 cannelloni in one layer. Coat the bottom lightly with Bechamel Sauce. Arrange cannelloni side by side over sauce and cover with remaining sauce. Dot with remaining 2 tablespoons butter.

9 Bake for 20 minutes, or until lightly browned and bubbly. Serve hot.

Vegetables Rolled in Crepes

SERVES 4 TO 6 (MAKES 12 ROLLS)

12 very thin slices Black Forest ham,
 fat trimmed
12 very thin 1½ × 4-inch slices
 Gruyère cheese
12 Crepes (page 268)
2 small carrots, cut into 6 × ¼-inch
 strips
12 asparagus spears, each 6 inches long
2 celery stalks (from heart), cut into
 6 × ¼-inch strips

12 small green onions (white part
 only), thinly sliced lengthwise
1 medium-size red or green long frying
 pepper, cored, seeded, and cut into
 thin strips
salt
freshly ground pepper
Quick Tomato Sauce (page 259)
Bechamel Sauce (page 255)

1 Place 1 slice of ham and 1 slice of cheese in center of a crepe. Add 2 carrot strips, 1 asparagus spear, 1 celery strip, 2 or 3 pieces green onion, 2 strips of pepper, and salt and pepper to taste. Fold over crepe and place in a large baking dish seam side down. Repeat with remaining crepes.

2 Cover first with tomato (but not completely), then add bechamel sauce, but not overall. Some tomato and some bechamel should show, as well as some of the crepes. Bake in preheated 400°F oven for 20 minutes or until hot and bubbly. Serve right away.

Lentils in Swiss Chard Rolls

SERVES 10 TO 12

48 squares (each 4 × 4 inches) Swiss
  chard leaves
2 tablespoons olive oil
1 cup thinly sliced green onions
1 cup cooked lentils
2 large fresh tomatoes, cored,
  blanched, peeled, seeded, and
  chopped (or 1 cup canned tomato
  pulp after putting through food mill)
1 cup raw long-grain rice

3 garlic cloves, finely chopped
1 cup chopped fresh parsley
1 tablespoon chopped fresh oregano or
  1 teaspoon dried
juice of 1 lemon
salt
freshly ground pepper
2 cups (about) chicken stock or
  vegetable broth

1 Wash Swiss chard squares in cool water, drain them and place in a large saucepan. Pour 2 quarts hot water over the leaves and drain almost immediately (the object here is simply to soften the leaves, to make them easy to roll). Dry the leaves and lay them on a flat surface glossy side down; unless you have a very large work surface, you will likely have to prepare these in batches.

2 Heat oil in a large skillet and sauté the green onions for a few minutes just to soften. Remove from heat and add the lentils, tomatoes, rice, garlic, ½ cup parsley, oregano, and lemon juice. Season to taste with salt and pepper. Mix well and place a level tablespoon on each leaf square. Roll and arrange stuffed leaves seam side down in a large, shallow flameproof pan with a cover. Barely cover them with stock or broth and bring to a boil. Lower heat, cover, and cook for 25 minutes. Remove from heat, let stand for 10 minutes or so, sprinkle remaining ½ cup parsley overall and serve.

Savoy Cabbage Rolls

SERVES 6

Many tasty vegetables rolled in Savoy cabbage leaves.

17 Savoy cabbage leaves, large leaves
  cut crosswise, to make about 24 pieces
2 tablespoons vegetable oil
1 cup chopped onion
1 cup drained canned chickpeas,
  mashed
½ cup fresh or frozen green peas
½ cup raw long-grain rice
½ cup chopped Virginia ham

2 large fresh tomatoes, cored,
  blanched, peeled, seeded, and
  chopped, or 1 cup canned tomatoes,
  put through a food mill
2 garlic cloves, finely chopped
½ cup chopped fresh parsley
1 teaspoon whole caraway seed
juice of 1 lemon
salt
freshly ground pepper
2 cups (about) Chicken Stock (page 251)

1 Cook 3 or 4 cabbage leaves at a time in boiling water for 8 minutes or until almost tender. Remove leaves with a slotted spoon, drain well and pat dry. Remove coarse ribs to make leaves easier to roll.

2 Heat oil in large saucepan and sauté onion until translucent. Remove from heat and add mashed chickpeas, green peas, rice, ham, tomatoes, garlic, ¼ cup parsley, caraway, and lemon juice. Toss well and season to taste with salt and pepper.

3 Arrange 5 or 6 leaves on a flat surface and put a heaping tablespoon of filling at the base of each leaf. Roll, fold over sides, and repeat with remaining leaves. Set rolls seam side down in a large, fairly shallow, flameproof casserole or skillet with tight-fitting cover. Add chicken stock to barely cover rolls. Season with additional pepper. Cover and simmer for 50 minutes, then remove from heat and let rolls stand for 10 minutes before serving. Sprinkle remaining ¼ cup parsley overall.

Cold Eggplant Rolls with Piquant Sauce

SERVES 4

2 small eggplants, about 12 ounces each
salt
½ cup olive oil
1 head curly endive
4 ounces smoked mozzarella (four
   2 × 3 × ¼-inch slices)

SAUCE
(makes about 1 cup)
½ cup olive oil
¼ cup red wine vinegar
1 anchovy filet
2 garlic cloves, finely chopped
¼ cup chopped fresh parsley
2 tablespoons finely chopped shallot
2 tablespoons capers
freshly ground pepper

1 Cut the ends off eggplants but leave them unpeeled. Stand each eggplant on its wide end and cut it lengthwise into the thinnest possible slices. Salt each slice lightly, lay the slices flat in a colander, and allow them to drain for 20 to 30 minutes. Dry each slice with a paper towel.

2 Heat 2 tablespoons olive oil in a large skillet and sauté the first batch of eggplant slices on both sides until they are cooked through. Some edges can char, but don't allow entire slice to blacken; the taste will be spoiled and it will be difficult to roll. Don't add more oil to skillet until you are ready to sauté the next batch of slices. As you remove each slice, roll it and set it aside to cool.

3 For sauce, combine olive oil and vinegar, add the anchovy, and mash it. Add the garlic, parsley, shallot, capers, and pepper to taste. Put the eggplant rolls on a large plate and spoon the sauce over them.

4 Discard any tough or frayed endive leaves. Separate remaining leaves and immerse in cool water. Leave for 10 minutes to crisp, then spin dry. Divide the best leaves among 4 plates. Arrange eggplant rolls on leaves, spooning sauce over. Cut mozzarella into 3 × ¼-inch strips and divide among plates. Serve at room temperature.

Opposite: Vegetable Salad à la Russe (page 202).

8

STOVE TOP AND BAKED VEGETABLES

The melding of vegetable flavors can be easily accomplished by cooking various vegetables together to make a composite dish, either in the oven or on top of the stove. Artichokes or asparagus, endive or eggplant, tomatoes or turnips cooked this way steam in their own aromatic juices. Vegetables may be combined for a variety of reasons: to add more liquid, thereby ending up with just the right amount of moistness; for compatible flavors (some vegetables seem absolutely made for each other); and, to achieve interesting textures.

In many of the following preparations, richly flavored vegetables such as onions, garlic, mushrooms, and carrots, not to mention a multitude of herbs, are mixed in various combinations. Though not always labeled *persillade, duxelles,* or *mirepoix,* you may notice that the essential ingredients of these classic flavoring preparations crop up from time to time.

Most of these recipes call for fresh vegetables. Use them whenever you can, resorting to frozen or canned goods only when it is impossible to find the fresh. It continues to amaze us how important this is; only a short while ago we used frozen carrots in a recipe instead of fresh and, honestly, the result was just not the same. Even home-frozen or preserved produce shows some damage, because blanching before freezing is essential but the vegetable's texture is bound to pay the price. As for canning, we've often found the result — including our own — to be overcooked. How can the poor vegetable survive in that fast and furious boiling water?

As we said in the introduction, this is not a vegetarian cookbook, but we believe vegetarians should have it. In this chapter surprisingly few recipes call for meat, and we hope the vegetarian reader will concentrate on the many simple yet interesting all-vegetable preparations. You will have many enjoyable hours (really moments) in the kitchen, let alone fabulous meals, by concocting your own vegetable plates — the combinations are never-ending.

Remember, in many parts of the world vegetables are considered more important than meat and receive very special attention. As you prepare and cook your vegetables, taste them all — taste them raw, partially cooked, and sometimes overcooked. In this way you'll see what is happening along the way. The taste of many raw vegetables is totally different from that of the cooked version, and without tasting you'll be as lost as in the lover's tunnel at Coney Island. But perhaps you enjoy that, too!

Spaghetti Squash with Spinach, Shallots, and Brandy

SERVES 4

Spaghetti squash is becoming popular, and here is a good way to prepare it. See photo 2 following page 172.

2 to 3 pounds spaghetti squash	2 tablespoons brandy
2 cups shredded fresh spinach leaves plus 8 large uncooked leaves	1 cup whipping cream
juice of 1 lemon	salt
5 tablespoons butter	freshly ground pepper
1 garlic clove, finely chopped	6 bacon slices, cooked until crisp, drained, and crumbled
2 tablespoons finely chopped shallots	1/4 cup freshly grated Parmesan cheese
1 cup thinly sliced mushrooms	

1 Halve the spaghetti squash lengthwise and remove the seeds. Place the squash in a large pot with 3 inches of water, cover, and boil for 25 minutes or until tender. Remove the spaghetti squash with a large spoon. Let cool slightly. Run a fork over the inside of the squash to release the flesh; it will resemble spaghetti strands (there should be about 2 cups).

2 Cook the shredded spinach in boiling salted water for about 3 minutes, or until tender. Drain well, add lemon juice, mix and set aside.

3 Melt the butter in a large skillet, add the garlic and shallots, and cook for 3 minutes. Add the mushrooms and cook an additional 5 minutes. Add the brandy and cream and bring the mixture to a boil. Remove from heat and add the spaghetti squash and spinach. Salt and pepper liberally and add the bacon bits and Parmesan cheese. Toss well.

4 Place two spinach leaves on each serving plate and top with spaghetti squash mixture. Serve right away.

Vegetable Curry

🍎

SERVES 6

This is a beautiful and tasty dish. Be sure to arrange the cooked vegetables attractively — put them in a baking dish or in any attractive container that can be put in the oven. Serve the rich, thick curry sauce in a separate bowl and ladle or spoon it over the vegetables as they are divided among individual plates. You can vary the vegetables as you wish, but keep colors in mind. For example, don't substitute turnips for carrots, or all the vegetables will be white. Remember too that green vegetables such as broccoli or Brussels sprouts will not fare well here. The curry sauce freezes well, so make enough to have some to freeze.

2 tablespoons vegetable oil
8 slices bacon
½ cup thinly sliced celery with leaves
½ cup finely chopped onion
3 garlic cloves, finely chopped
½ cup all-purpose flour
2 apples, peeled, seeded, and sliced
¼ cup curry powder
6 tablespoons tomato paste
2 tablespoons sugar
2 tablespoons fresh lemon juice
3 cups rich chicken stock
½ to 1 cup light cream
2 cups carrots cut diagonally into
   1-inch-thick pieces
1½ pounds very small new potatoes,
   cooked and peeled
2 cups cauliflower flowerets (about
   1-inch size), cooked until tender,
   drained, and patted dry

1 cup 1-inch celery pieces, steamed
   until crisp-tender, drained, and
   patted dry

CONDIMENTS
crumbled bacon pieces
1 cup chopped onion
1 cup chopped green bell pepper
1 cup small fresh pineapple chunks
1 cup shredded coconut
1 cup sliced bananas (tossed in lemon
   juice)
½ cup crushed peanuts (use a rolling
   pin)
1 cup cored, blanched, peeled, seeded,
   and diced fresh tomatoes
1 cup diced apples (tossed in lemon juice)
1½ cups Peach and Almond Chutney

1 Heat oil in a large saucepan and sauté the bacon slices until well done. Remove them with a slotted spoon, drain on a paper towel, and set aside. (Crumble later, put in a bowl, and serve as condiment.)

2 Add the celery, onion, and garlic and sauté for 5 minutes. Add flour and cook, stirring constantly, for 2 minutes. Add the apples, curry powder, tomato paste, sugar, lemon juice, and stock and cook 45 minutes; stir frequently to keep bottom from scorching. Taste. If you prefer stronger, combine additional curry powder with several tablespoons of leftover stock and add to the sauce. Process through a food mill. You should have about 5 cups sauce.

3 Add light cream to sauce, starting with ½ cup and adding more if you want it thinner (this should be quite a thick sauce). Bring to a boil and turn off heat. Arrange the vegetables in an ovenproof dish and put in 375°F oven to heat through. Transfer the curry sauce to a serving dish and set it in the center of the table, surrounded with bowls or saucers of the condiments.

Peach and Almond Chutney

MAKES ABOUT 3 PINTS

5 cups sliced fresh peaches or two
 1-pound packages frozen
 unsweetened peach slices
¼ cup fresh lemon juice
¼ cup finely chopped lemon zest
1 cup golden raisins
½ cup water

½ cup raspberry vinegar
⅔ cup firmly packed brown sugar
⅔ cup slivered toasted almonds
½ cup peeled and finely chopped fresh
 ginger root or preserved ginger
1 large red bell pepper, cored, seeded,
 and finely chopped

1 Blanch and peel the fresh peaches. Cut them in half and discard the pits. Cut the peach halves into 1-inch slices; you should have about 5 cups. (If using frozen peaches, simply add them to the other ingredients straight from the packages; no thawing is necessary.)

2 Combine all ingredients in a heavy enameled saucepan, stir well, and bring to a boil. Lower the heat and simmer slowly for 1 hour, or until chutney is as thick as you want it. Let cool and refrigerate until ready to use. Or if you wish, divide chutney among sterilized jars, process in boiling water bath and store in a cool, dark place.

Vegetable Lasagna

SERVES 8

The pasta is given a tremendous lift with all these vegetables and herbs. If you like lasagna, you'll like this one. See photo 4 following page 172.

6 small zucchini (about 1 × 6 inches), washed, ends trimmed, and partly peeled
salt
14 lasagna noodles, approximately 2 × 9 inches, preferably homemade
vegetable oil for sautéing
2 garlic cloves, halved
6 green frying peppers, cored, seeded, and cut into 1-inch lengths
½ large red bell pepper, cored, seeded, and cut into ¼-inch-thick strips

2 large onions, thinly sliced
2 cups Velouté Sauce (page 256)
8 ounces mozzarella cheese, shredded
½ cup freshly grated Parmesan cheese
12 fresh plum tomatoes, cored, blanched, peeled, and seeded, or one 28-ounce can plum tomatoes, drained and seeded
8 fresh basil leaves, finely chopped
18 large asparagus spears, cooked

1 Cut zucchini lengthwise into 4 pieces. Place in colander and sprinkle liberally with salt. Let drain 30 to 60 minutes. Pat dry with paper towels.

2 Cook lasagna noodles in boiling water until slightly underdone, about 8 minutes. Drain carefully, lay on cloth toweling and dry.

3 Heat 2 tablespoons oil in a large skillet. Sauté 2 garlic halves until golden and discard. Sauté green peppers in batches, adding more oil as necessary.

4 In same skillet, do the same with the zucchini slices, red pepper, and onions, adding more oil as needed and sautéing and discarding remaining garlic in between.

5 Spread thin layer of Velouté Sauce in 8 × 11 × 2-inch glass or ceramic baking dish. Add 3 lasagna strips and then some zucchini, green pepper, onion, mozzarella, and Parmesan.

6 Top with 3 more lasagna strips. Add a little Velouté Sauce, some of each cheese, and all the tomatoes. Sprinkle with most of the basil, reserving a little for garnish, and then a bit more of both cheeses.

7 Add 3 more lasagna strips and a little more Velouté Sauce. Top with 12 asparagus spears, remaining zucchini, green peppers, and onions, and more cheese, but reserve some of each cheese for topping.

8 Add 3 more lasagna strips and the remaining Velouté. Arrange remaining 6 asparagus spears in spoke fashion on top with tips pointing inward. Sprinkle fried red peppers overall. Top with remaining cheeses and basil.

9 Cover with foil and bake in preheated 375°F oven for 40 minutes, or until bubbly, removing foil after 30 minutes. Bake 10 minutes more and, if top is not browned, run under broiler for a few minutes. Let lasagna stand for 10 to 15 minutes after removing from oven.

Fennel and Potato Stew

SERVES 4

Fennel is a fragrant vegetable we should use more often.

½ cup corn or vegetable oil
4 small new potatoes (about 8 ounces),
   peeled and cut into ½-inch cubes
1 large fennel bulb, cut into ¼-inch
   slices and then into ¼-inch sticks,
   including some leaves

1 cup chicken stock or vegetable broth
1 tablespoon finely chopped orange zest
salt
freshly ground pepper
1 cup fresh or frozen peas (if fresh,
   cook until tender; if frozen, thaw)

1 Heat oil in a saucepan, add cubed potatoes, and cook until they begin to soften, about 5 minutes. Add fennel and cook another 5 minutes. Add stock or broth, orange zest, salt, and pepper, bring to a boil, lower heat and cook 30 minutes, until fennel is tender but not overdone.

2 Add peas and cook for several minutes longer. Serve hot.

Risotto Primavera

SERVES 6

See photo 2 following page 108.

2½ quarts chicken stock or vegetable
    broth
8 ounces small zucchini (1 × 5 inches)
8 ounces green beans
8 ounces carrots
8 ounces snow peas
6 medium mushrooms

12 tablespoons (1½ sticks) butter
3 cups Arborio rice
½ cup whipping cream
1 cup freshly grated Parmesan cheese
¼ cup finely chopped flat-leaf parsley
freshly ground pepper
salt (optional)

1 Bring the stock or broth to a boil in a large saucepan. Lower the heat and keep it at the lowest possible simmer.

2 Trim ends from zucchini, green beans, carrots, and snow peas. Wash and dry vegetables. Slice zucchini and carrots diagonally into ½-inch pieces. Slice green beans and snow peas diagonally into 1-inch pieces. Clean and slice the mushrooms.

3 Melt 8 tablespoons (1 stick) butter in another saucepan and sauté the zucchini, carrots, and green beans for 4 minutes, tossing frequently. Add snow peas and mushrooms and sauté for 1 minute. Add rice and cook for 2 minutes, stirring to coat all the rice with butter.

4 Add 1 cup hot stock or broth to the rice and vegetable mixture. Cook and stir gently for several minutes until the liquid is absorbed. Repeat with 5 more cups of stock, *1 cup at a time*, stirring gently all the while until each cup of liquid is absorbed. Continue adding stock about ½ cup at a time until liquid is absorbed. When all the stock has been absorbed, add the remaining 4 tablespoons butter, cut into pieces, and the cream. Remove from heat and add ⅔ of the Parmesan and parsley. Season with pepper and toss lightly. Add salt if needed. Sprinkle remaining Parmesan and parsley on top and serve.

Vegetable Ricotta Custard

SERVES 4

Vegetables in custard make a very good lunch or supper entree or a perfect buffet item. This dish is easy to make.

12 small white boiling onions, peeled
2 tablespoons unsalted butter
1 celery stalk, thinly sliced
1 carrot, thinly sliced
½ cup fresh or frozen green peas
¼ cup dry vermouth
6 eggs

1 cup whipping cream
1 tablespoon all-purpose flour
1 cup whole-milk ricotta
½ cup freshly grated Parmesan cheese
freshly ground pepper
1 tablespoon finely chopped green onion
1 tablespoon finely chopped fresh parsley

1 Put onions in a saucepan, cover with water and bring to a boil. Lower heat and simmer for about 5 minutes or until tender. Drain onions and cool by running cold water over them.

2 Melt the butter in another saucepan and sauté the celery and carrot for about 5 minutes or until tender. Add the onions, peas, and vermouth and bring to a boil. Lower heat, cover and simmer for 5 minutes.

3 Lightly beat the eggs in a large bowl with the cream. Add flour and beat until smooth. Add ricotta, Parmesan, and pepper to taste and blend well. Add the cooked vegetables with a slotted spoon, reserving the cooking liquid; mix well. If the reserved cooking liquid is thin, boil it over moderately high heat until it has thickened slightly and stir it into the mixture.

4 Pour the custard into a well-buttered 1½-quart baking dish and bake in preheated 375°F oven for 30 to 35 minutes, or until set. Let the custard stand for 3 minutes. Sprinkle with green onion and parsley and serve.

Zucchini Pudding

SERVES 4 TO 6

This is a custard most delicately flavored with fresh zucchini. Serve within 10 minutes of removing from the oven, or it will begin to sink. Accompany the pudding with a salad of Belgian endive and top with sprays of watercress.

4 medium zucchini
1 tablespoon salt
1 fresh hot green or red pepper, finely chopped
¼ cup finely chopped fresh basil or 1 teaspoon dried

3 eggs, room temperature
¼ cup all-purpose flour
2 tablespoons butter, melted
2 cups light cream

1 Wash the zucchini and trim off the ends, but do not peel. Shred the zucchini on the large holes of a grater. Transfer it to a colander and layer with salt. Let the liquid drain from the zucchini for about 30 minutes. With your hands, press down on the zucchini in the colander to remove as much liquid as possible. Transfer the zucchini to a bowl.

2 Add the chopped pepper and basil, and toss with the zucchini. Beat the eggs and cream together and stir into the zucchini mixture, then stir in flour. Blend in the melted butter.

3 Pour the mixture into a buttered 1½-quart glass or ceramic baking dish. Place the baking dish in a pan of hot water. Bake in a preheated 325°F oven for 1 hour, or until firm.

Baked Cauliflower with Carrots, Onions, and Sour Cream

SERVES 6

This is one of the simplest dishes in the book, and one of our favorites. It is vegetables at their best.

4 tablespoons (½ stick) butter
2 pounds small new potatoes, boiled in
    jackets until tender, drained,
    cooled, peeled, and cut into ¼-inch
    slices
6 eggs, hard-cooked, shelled, and sliced
1 cauliflower including greens (about
    2 pounds), cored, cut into flowerets,
    sliced ½ inch thick, and cooked

3 carrots, peeled, cut diagonally into
    ½-inch-thick slices, and cooked
2 onions, sliced and cooked
1 cup sour cream
¼ cup Dijon mustard
1½ cups rich chicken stock or vegetable
    broth
1 teaspoon dill seed

1 Using 2 tablespoons of butter, liberally butter an oval 14 × 9½ × 2-inch (3-quart) glass or ceramic dish and arrange potato slices on bottom.

2 Arrange the eggs at even intervals over potatoes. Fill in around eggs with cooked cauliflower, carrots, and onions. Dot with remaining butter.

3 In a bowl combine ½ cup sour cream, 2 tablespoons mustard, stock or broth, and dill seed and whisk until well blended. Taste and adjust seasoning.

4 Pour sauce over vegetables and eggs, cover with foil, and bake in preheated 375°F oven for 1 hour. Remove cover and bake 30 minutes more.

5 In another bowl, combine ½ cup sour cream, 2 tablespoons mustard, and salt and pepper to taste. Blend thoroughly. Add a good dollop of sour cream/mustard sauce to each serving of vegetables.

Yellow Pepper Risotto

SERVES 2

Yellow peppers, not as common as their green and red sisters, have a lot of flavor.

2 tablespoons unsalted butter
1 small to medium onion, finely
 chopped (about ½ cup)
1 large yellow bell pepper (about
 8 ounces), cored, seeded, and cut
 into ¼-inch cubes

1½ cups chicken stock or vegetable
 broth, heated
½ cup Arborio rice
¼ teaspoon freshly grated nutmeg
salt
freshly ground pepper
¼ cup grated pecorino Romano cheese

1 Melt butter in a saucepan or casserole over moderate heat. Sauté onion and pepper for about 6 minutes, or until onion begins to turn translucent.

2 Add ⅓ of the heated stock and the rice, stirring so all rice is coated with liquid. Stir every minute or so, and when rice has absorbed the liquid add another ⅓ cup stock or broth; again stir and allow rice to absorb liquid. Add another ⅓ cup stock, let rice absorb the liquid, and finally add remaining stock.

3 Add nutmeg, salt, and pepper and keep stirring. When liquid is absorbed, remove from heat and stir in 3 tablespoons cheese. Top with remaining tablespoon of cheese and pass more. Serve immediately.

Couscous à l'Abdul

SERVES 6 TO 8

On a recent trip to Morocco we were delighted with the array of fresh vegetables in the markets and on the dining table. The freshness and abundance of vegetables is best seen in this most popular North African dish. It is traditionally cooked in a *couscoussière* — something like a double boiler with a perforated top — but special equipment is not essential, as in the U.S. most couscous is of the quick-cooking variety. Couscous is precooked semolina (as in pasta) made from durum wheat. Moroccan couscous is accented with saffron, Tunisians add ginger and chili pepper, and the Algerians thicken their sauce with tomato puree. But in each case the dish is a festival of vegetables.

Abdullah Meskine, our good and kind friend in Fez, is largely responsible for our acquaintance with this dish.

2 turnips, cut into ¾-inch cubes (1 cup)
4 medium to large potatoes, peeled
   and cut into 1-inch chunks
   (2 generous cups)
2 cups baby carrots
2 cups butternut squash cut into
   ¾-inch cubes
4 small zucchini (about 1 × 6 inches),
   ends trimmed, cut into ¾-inch
   pieces (about 2 cups)
1 large green bell pepper, cored,
   seeded, and cut into 1-inch squares
1 teaspoon saffron threads, crumbled
8 tablespoons (1 stick) butter
3 cups water
1 pound couscous (about 3 cups) (see
   note)

2 tablespoons orange flower water
½ teaspoon ground cloves
½ teaspoon cinnamon

SAUCE
1 tablespoon olive oil
2 tablespoons butter
2 pounds boneless lamb, cut into
   1-inch chunks
2 large onions, coarsely chopped
2 teaspoons salt
freshly ground pepper
¼ cup tomato paste
½ teaspoon turmeric
pinch of red pepper flakes
1 cup water
2 or 3 beef hind shank bones

1 Heat oil and butter in a large skillet and brown lamb pieces. Transfer to a large saucepan or stockpot. Add onions to skillet and cook until translucent. Add salt, pepper, tomato paste, turmeric, and red pepper flakes (this will be a very thick mixture). Cook for 3 to 4 minutes, stirring frequently, and transfer to saucepan with meat. Deglaze skillet with a cup of water and transfer to saucepan.

2 Add bones to saucepan and cover all with water. Bring to a boil, lower heat, and simmer for 40 minutes or until lamb pieces are tender and may be pierced with a fork.

3 Clean and prepare all vegetables, but keep them separated as they will go into the sauce at different times.

4 Add turnips first and cook for 10 minutes. Next add potatoes and carrots and cook another 10 minutes. Add butternut squash, zucchini, green pepper, and saffron and cook 20 minutes (vegetables should be tender; if not, cook a little longer). Remove and discard bones.

5 Meanwhile, combine butter and water in large covered saucepan and heat until water boils and butter is melted. Add couscous all at once, cover, and immediately remove from heat. Let stand, covered, for 4 to 5 minutes or until all liquid is absorbed.

6 Turn out couscous onto large, deep serving platter. Sprinkle with orange flower water, cloves, and cinnamon. Toss lightly but thoroughly to distribute flavors and to fluff couscous. Form a mound, make a depression in center, and add vegetables and meat; spoon some more around the couscous on outer edge of platter. Put remaining sauce and any remaining vegetables in a bowl and pass it, as more sauce will be needed. Make individual servings from the large platter; this dish does not lend itself to individual plate servings.

NOTE
Cracked wheat, kasha, or cracked millet can be substituted for couscous.

New Potatoes and Other Vegetables with Yogurt and Cheddar Cheese

SERVES 4

This light, refreshing, and healthy vegetable garden dish was created by Joanne Pattison, a highly regarded physiologist.

1 pound small new potatoes
1 pint (2 cups) plain yogurt
½ cup thinly sliced green onions
½ cup cored, blanched, peeled, seeded, and chopped fresh tomato
1 cup sliced cauliflower flowerets

1 cup thinly sliced carrots
1 cup sliced broccoli flowerets
¼ cup chopped onion
½ cup chopped red bell pepper
1½ cups finely shredded sharp Cheddar cheese

1 Scrub potatoes and boil until tender. Split in half and arrange in serving dish cut side up.

2 Combine yogurt, green onions, and tomato. Mix well and pour over potatoes.

3 Cook cauliflower, carrots, and broccoli separately until barely tender. Drain and pat dry. Arrange on top of dressed potatoes.

4 Sprinkle onion, red bell pepper, and cheese overall. The dish requires no further cooking. Serve as is with crusty bread, and finish off with sherbet and fresh fruit.

Burdock with Olive Oil

SERVES 2

1 pound burdock stalks, prepared
  according to directions on page 21
¼ cup olive oil
2 large garlic cloves, peeled and halved
salt
freshly ground pepper

1 After cleaning burdock stalks, cut into 2- or 3-inch lengths. Put in boiling salted water and cook until tender, about 8 to 10 minutes. Drain and set aside.

2 Heat oil in a large skillet and sauté garlic until just beginning to brown. Remove and discard. Add cooked burdock stems and sauté for 5 minutes, until heated through completely. Salt and pepper to taste and serve hot.

Vegetable Pot Pie with a Little Chicken

SERVES 4

This is our variation of the classic chicken pot pie, with the emphasis on the vegetables.

1½ cups all-purpose flour
1 teaspoon baking powder
½ teaspoon salt
5 tablespoons chilled unsalted butter,
   cut into very small pieces
1 tablespoon chilled shortening
1 teaspoon dried chervil
3 tablespoons ice water
3 cups chicken stock
2 whole chicken breasts with ribs
3 large carrots, cut into 1-inch pieces
8 boiling onions, peeled
1 cup sugar snap peas, cut into 2-inch
   pieces

1 cup sliced mushrooms
¼ cup dry white wine or dry vermouth
6 tablespoons (¾ stick) unsalted butter
6 tablespoons all-purpose flour
2 cups chicken stock, heated
½ cup whipping cream
salt
freshly ground pepper
pinch of mace
1 tablespoon chopped fresh tarragon or
   1 teaspoon dried
1 egg white, beaten to soft peaks

1 Combine 1½ cups flour, baking powder, salt, chilled butter, shortening, and chervil in a large mixing bowl and mix with pastry blender or fingertips until the mixture resembles coarse meal. Add the ice water and quickly gather the dough into a ball. Knead the dough a few times. Sprinkle lightly with flour. Wrap the dough in waxed paper and refrigerate for 1 hour.

2 Place 3 cups chicken stock in a large saucepan. Let it come to a boil and add the breasts. Lower the heat and cook for 15 minutes or until tender. Transfer the chicken to a bowl to cool.

3 Steam the carrots and onions in another saucepan for 15 minutes. Remove the vegetables and set aside. Add the sugar snap peas, steam for 3 minutes, and set aside.

4 In a small saucepan combine the mushrooms and the wine or vermouth and simmer for 5 minutes, or until wine is absorbed.

5 In a 3-quart saucepan melt 6 tablespoons butter and add 6 tablespoons flour. Blend well with a wire whisk. Slowly add 2 cups of heated chicken stock. Stir constantly for about 15 minutes or until sauce is thickened. Add the cream and slowly bring to a boil. Remove from heat and season with salt, pepper, and mace.

6 Remove the chicken from the bones in large pieces. Place meat in a 2-quart round casserole along with the carrots, onions, mushrooms, peas, tarragon, and salt and pepper to taste. Stir lightly. Add 2 cups sauce and taste for seasoning.

7 Preheat oven to 400°F. On a lightly floured surface, roll out the dough ⅛ inch thick and cut to fit the casserole with a ½-inch overhang. Carefully place the dough over the casserole. Tuck the overhang under and crimp the edge; be sure to press to the rim of the casserole to seal. Using leftover dough cut out some leaf shapes (or whatever design you wish) and decorate the top. Cut a few slits in the middle of the pie to allow steam to escape. Brush the top with the egg white. Bake for 45 to 50 minutes, or until crust is golden and filling bubbles through the slits. Serve hot.

Okra and Cornmeal Pudding with Old-Fashioned Spicy Tomato Sauce

SERVES 6

See photo 2 following page 124.

8 ounces small young okra, stemmed
    and cut crosswise into ¼-inch slices
6 cups water
1 teaspoon salt
2 cups yellow cornmeal

4 tablespoons (½ stick) unsalted butter,
    cut into ¼-inch cubes
2 to 3 cups Old-Fashioned Spicy
    Tomato Sauce (page 258)

1 Put the okra in a glass or ceramic bowl until ready to use.

2 Bring the water to boil in a saucepan. Add the salt and okra, cover pan, and cook over low heat for 8 minutes. Remove cover, raise heat, and very slowly add cornmeal while stirring with a wooden spoon. Lower heat after all cornmeal has been added and stir constantly until mixture is very thick, about 6 minutes or a bit longer. Mixture should be smooth.

3 Remove from heat and add the butter pieces, reserving a few to butter a heatproof round or oval 1½-quart dish. Mix in butter and transfer cornmeal mixture to buttered dish. Spread and pat into dish with wooden spoon. Let rest 2 minutes, then turn it out onto serving plate.

4 Serve pudding immediately with Spicy Tomato Sauce on the side.

Boston Baked Beans

SERVES 6

1 pound dried Great Northern beans
  (2 cups)
2 quarts water
1 medium onion, finely chopped
2 tablespoons ketchup
1 tablespoon cider vinegar
2 teaspoons dry mustard

¼ cup dark molasses
1 teaspoon curry powder
1 tablespoon Worcestershire sauce
⅔ cup firmly packed dark brown sugar
4 ounces salt pork, cut into 3-inch cubes
salt
freshly ground pepper

1 Wash the beans several times in cold water and pick over to remove any foreign particles, pebbles, and floating beans. Drain beans. In a 3-quart casserole or saucepan combine beans and 2 quarts water. Bring to a quick boil and cook for 2 minutes. Turn off the heat, cover the casserole, and let the beans soak for 1 hour.

2 Bring the beans back to a boil, lower the heat, and simmer 30 minutes. Drain the beans over a large bowl and save the cooking liquid.

3 Return the beans to the casserole. In a small bowl combine 1 cup of the reserved liquid, the onion, ketchup, vinegar, dry mustard, molasses, curry powder, Worcestershire sauce, brown sugar, salt pork, and salt and pepper. Mix well with a wooden spoon, pour over the beans in the casserole, and stir well.

4 Preheat oven to 250°F. Cover the casserole and bake the beans for 7 to 8 hours. After 4 hours check the beans; if they are too dry, add ½ to 1 cup of the reserved cooking liquid. For the last 30 minutes of cooking remove the cover; bake until all liquid is evaporated.

Assorted Vegetable Plates

Each of the following recipes presents a special way to cook one specific vegetable, or sometimes two together, with the purpose of combining several into a vegetable plate. Rearrange the combinations if you wish, keeping the texture, color, and taste of each vegetable in mind.

PLATTER 1

Pearl Onions and Baby Carrots

SERVES 4

Pearl onions are delicious by themselves, but even more so when united with small whole carrots.

> *8 ounces fresh pearl onions*
> *8 ounces baby carrots*
> *1 cup water*
> *3 tablespoons butter*
> *2 teaspoons sugar*
> *salt*
> *freshly ground pepper*

1 Peel the onions, wash and dry them. Trim ends from carrots and brush them clean under cool water; pat dry. Put onions and carrots in a saucepan with the water and 1 tablespoon butter. Cook over moderate heat until vegetables are tender and most of the water has evaporated.

2 Add the remaining butter and sugar and toss. Cook until vegetables just begin to color. Season to taste with salt and pepper. Serve hot.

White Potatoes Baked in Cream

SERVES 4

This is one of the best ways to prepare potatoes; they are perfect by themselves or with other vegetables.

2 pounds white boiling potatoes
4 tablespoons (½ stick) butter
2 garlic cloves, minced
salt
freshly ground pepper
2 cups whipping cream

1 Peel the potatoes and slice them as thinly as you can. As soon as they are peeled and sliced, put them in cool water and let stand for 15 minutes or so. Drain and dry well in cotton toweling.

2 Butter an 8 × 8 × 2-inch baking dish with about 1 tablespoon butter. Arrange a layer of potatoes in it. Sprinkle a little of the minced garlic overall, dot with butter, season with salt and pepper, and repeat until all potatoes, garlic, and butter are used. Be sure you have buttered top layer.

3 Heat cream but do not let it boil. Pour over potatoes. Bake in pre-heated 375°F oven for about 40 minutes or until potatoes are tender. Most of the cream will have been absorbed by the potatoes; cover with foil during baking if you think potatoes are becoming too dry. When done, run under broiler to give potatoes a golden glow.

Sautéed Chinese Long Beans

SERVES 4

1 pound Chinese long beans
6 tablespoons (¾ stick) butter
½ cup thinly sliced green onions
salt
freshly ground pepper
1 tablespoon white wine vinegar

1 Wash the beans and cut them into thirds (the beans are at least 12 inches long, so you'll have 4- to 5-inch pieces). Cook them in boiling salted water for about 8 minutes after the water has returned to the boil; do not overcook. Drain and dry beans well in cotton toweling.

2 Melt the butter in a large skillet and sauté the onions until they just begin to brown. Add the beans and sauté over moderately high heat. Season with salt and pepper, then sauté until beans begin to brown (this will only take a couple of minutes). Add vinegar to pan, toss well, and serve immediately.

❦

Zucchini Cups Filled with Radish Slivers

SERVES 4

2 small zucchini (about 1 × 6 inches)
4 long white radishes
8 red radishes
3 tablespoons vegetable, corn, or
  peanut oil

1 tablespoon white wine vinegar or
  fresh lemon juice
salt
freshly ground pepper
pinch of cayenne pepper

1 Wash zucchini and trim ends with a straight cut so each can stand on end. Cook in boiling salted water until tender. Drain and refresh in cold

164

water; dry well. Cut zucchini in half crosswise so each half can stand on end. Cut each half in half again with a diagonal cut; this will give you 4 pieces of zucchini, each with one flat, straight cut and one diagonal cut. Scoop out seeds from diagonal end to form a cup with straight bottom as base. Repeat with second zucchini. Salt and pepper each cup.

2 Shred white and red radishes. Combine oil, vinegar or lemon juice, salt, and pepper and mix into radish. Fill each cup to overflowing.

PLATTER 2

Baked Sweet Potatoes with Honey, Cream, and Orange Zest

SERVES 3 OR 6

7 tablespoons butter
3 large sweet potatoes, scrubbed and
  dried
6 tablespoons honey

6 tablespoons whipping cream
2 tablespoons finely chopped orange zest
salt
freshly ground pepper

1 Rub 1 teaspoon butter over each sweet potato, wrap in foil, and bake in 350°F oven until tender, about 1 to 1½ hours. Remove from oven and allow to cool somewhat, although a cotton towel or pot holder will help you handle the hot potato. Cut each sweet potato in half and scoop out inside. Working with one potato half at a time, mix pulp with 1 tablespoon each of butter and honey, ½ teaspoon orange zest, salt, and pepper. Return to potato skin. Repeat until all 6 halves have been emptied and refilled.

2 Arrange potato halves on a baking sheet and place in a preheated 375°F oven until very hot. Serve right away.

Lightly Sautéed Fiddlehead Ferns

SERVES 6

These vegetables, gaining in popularity, are now seen at many green-grocers. They grow in the eastern U.S. and are only available in early spring. Do not use tinned fiddlehead ferns, as they will not work in this dish.

2 pounds fiddlehead ferns
6 tablespoons clarified butter

1 In a large saucepan bring several quarts of salted water to boil. Put in fiddlehead ferns and cook for 5 minutes. Immediately drain and dry them in cotton toweling.

2 Heat butter in a large skillet until it begins to turn brown. Add the dried fiddleheads and sauté them for several minutes, turning them over carefully. Serve right away.

❧

Vegetable Bundles Vinaigrette

MAKES 12

See photo 1 opposite page 124.

1 large red bell pepper
12 snow peas
2 celery stalks
2 zucchini, each about 1 × 6 inches
24 green beans
2 large carrots

¾ cup olive oil
¼ cup white wine vinegar
½ teaspoon Dijon mustard
salt
freshly ground pepper
4 green onions

1 Core and seed bell pepper and slice into ¼-inch-thick strips. Cut into 2½-inch lengths. Set aside in bowl of ice water.

2 Cut snow peas and celery stalks into ¼ × 2½-inch strips. Add to bowl with pepper strips.

3 Trim ends from zucchini. Scrub squash but do not peel. Cut into strips the same size as other vegetables, discarding seedy centers. Steam until barely tender. Transfer to bowl with other vegetables.

4 Cut green beans and carrots into strips to match other vegetables. Steam each until tender and add to ice water bowl. Drain all vegetables and pat dry in cotton towels.

5 For vinaigrette, combine olive oil, vinegar, mustard, salt, and pepper and mix well. Toss with vegetables and marinate several hours at room temperature.

6 Trim green onions and carefully separate leaves, keeping them as long as possible (keep in mind that each leaf is to wrap a 1-inch bundle of vegetables). Put raw leaves in boiling water in a large skillet. Turn off heat immediately and transfer onion leaves to toweling.

7 Place one onion leaf on work surface and over it arrange a variety of vegetables to make a bundle about 1 inch in diameter. Wrap the bundle with the onion leaf, tying carefully or just wrapping leaf around bundle as far as it will stretch. Arrange on flat plate. When all bundles are made, pour any excess dressing over bundles to marinate further; or if you wish, put one or two bundles on each plate, top with dressing, and serve.

Tomatoes and Olives on Skewers

SERVES 6

18 cherry tomatoes, stemmed, washed,
*   and dried*
12 whole pitted olives
3 tablespoons butter, melted
salt
freshly ground pepper

1 If using wooden skewers (they should be at least 6 inches long), soak them in water for 20 to 30 minutes.

2 Skewer tomatoes and olives by first spearing a tomato, then an olive, next a tomato, another olive, and a third tomato. Repeat to make 6 skewers.

3 Lightly brush tomatoes and olives with butter on all sides. Season with salt and pepper. Broil 6 inches under flame; when just beginning to char, remove and serve.

PLATTER 3

Leeks Baked in Bechamel

SERVES 6

6 medium to large whole leeks,
*   washed carefully*
1 cup Bechamel Sauce (page 255)
½ cup shredded Swiss or Gruyère cheese
salt
freshly ground pepper
1 tablespoon butter

1 Place leeks in skillet large enough to hold them in one layer. Barely cover with water, add a bit of salt, and bring to boil. Cook 10 to 15 minutes, turning leeks once, until barely tender; do not overcook.

2 Spread ½ cup Bechamel Sauce on bottom of baking dish just large enough to hold leeks in one layer. Add leeks. Pour remaining sauce over the leeks, sprinkle the cheese overall and salt lightly, but be liberal with the pepper. Cut the butter into 8 pieces and dot top of leeks. Bake in preheated 375°F oven for 10 minutes or until sauce bubbles. If cheese doesn't brown on top, run under broiler for a minute or two.

Yellow Squash with Curried Walnuts

SERVES 6

Try yellow crookneck squash first, but another summer squash may be used in its place — for example, zucchini or scalloped pattypan. You can also use winter squashes such as butternut, but cut them into 1-inch cubes, boil until almost tender, and then sauté.

2 pounds yellow squash
1 tablespoon salt
6 tablespoons (¾ stick) butter
¼ cup vegetable oil
1 teaspoon curry powder
1 cup walnut meats, broken in half

1 Cut squash into ¼-inch slices and put in a colander. Sprinkle with salt and toss. Allow to drain for 15 minutes or so. Dry in cotton toweling.

2 In a large skillet, heat 2 tablespoons butter with 2 tablespoons oil and sauté one-half of the squash slices until they are tender and just begin to color (pierce them with a fork to test for tenderness). Transfer to paper toweling and add remaining 2 tablespoons butter and oil to skillet. Sauté remaining squash and transfer to toweling.

3 Melt remaining butter in same skillet, add curry and cook until thoroughly combined, about 2 to 3 minutes. Add the walnuts, toss to coat, and cook for several minutes until walnuts are toasted. Return squash slices to pan, turn up heat, and heat through, tossing frequently. Serve immediately.

❧

Eggplant Puffs

SERVES 6

The crisp outsides and soft insides of the eggplant cubes combine to make this a delectable dish. It is an excellent accompaniment to other vegetables.

2 medium eggplants	freshly ground pepper
2 tablespoons salt	3 eggs, well beaten
½ cup all-purpose flour	¼ cup milk
1 teaspoon salt	1 cup vegetable, corn, or peanut oil

1 Select fresh, firm eggplants; they should be young, tender, and not too seedy. Wipe them clean with kitchen toweling and slice off both ends; do not peel. Cut each eggplant into 1-inch cubes. Put all the cubes in a colander, sprinkle with 2 tablespoons salt, toss, and let stand for about 40 minutes to drain.

2 Combine the flour, 1 teaspoon salt, and a liberal amount of freshly ground pepper in a plastic bag. Add the eggplant cubes, close the bag and shake it vigorously to coat each piece.

3 Combine the eggs and milk in a shallow bowl and blend.

4 Heat the oil in a large skillet; it should be hot but not smoking. Dip several floured eggplant cubes into the egg mixture and put them in the skillet. Continue to add eggplant to skillet, but be sure to leave about ½ inch between cubes. Turn the cubes as they brown and puff on each side, about 2 minutes. Transfer eggplant to paper towels to drain. Although the cubes cook quickly and are best eaten right away, they will keep in a warm oven for about 30 minutes.

Finely Grated Raw Carrots with Watercress Sprays

SERVES 6

3 carrots
¼ cup vegetable oil
1 tablespoon raspberry vinegar
salt
freshly ground pepper
6 large watercress sprays

1 Trim ends of carrots and scrape with a vegetable peeler. Put through the finest food processor shredder.

2 Combine oil, vinegar, salt, and pepper. Blend thoroughly and pour over carrots. Toss well. Divide among 6 plates, mounding each portion. Top with a watercress spray.

9

CASSEROLES AND COVERED DISHES

Casserole cookery is popular all over, and entire books have been written on the subject. "Casserole" can mean two things: the actual cooking vessel, which is a container with a tight-fitting lid; or the process used for cooking food in it. The food may or may not include meats, grains, vegetables, or pasta; it may even include them all. The refinements of casserole cookery, such as *carbonnades, daubes, ragoûts,* and *estouffades,* usually involve braising or sautéing and are therefore actually combinations of cooking methods.

Opposite: Vegetable Lasagna (page 146).
Preceding page: Vegetable Bean Soup with
Pistou (page 222).

The term "casserole" these days is indeed broad—simply put, it includes any foods brought together, precooked or not, in the same vessel, and cooked in the oven or covered on top of the stove. Casseroles are among the most popular buffet items and can easily be expanded to feed large groups.

Casseroles are often prepared ahead of time, may be frozen cooked or sometimes uncooked, may be eaten cold, and are usually excellent when reheated and served again. No wonder, then, that everyone finds them tasty and time-saving food preparations. Good bread and bountiful salads are the best casserole accompaniments.

In making casseroles, remember their inherent self-basting action: steam condenses on the cover and drips back over the food, making the addition of much liquid unnecessary unless you are cooking rice. Most casseroles cook long and slowly, and the melding and condensation of flavors and juices give the dish body.

Almost nothing expresses a spirit of open-handed hospitality as well as a casserole dish when its cover is lifted off and the steam and aromas invade our senses. Everyone helps himself; everyone enjoys.

Mushroom Ragout

SERVES 4 TO 6

Artificially cultivated in sheds, cellars, and airy caves, mushrooms are abundant and available all through the year. This is a very tasty stew because the fresh mushrooms are accented with some dried ones.

4 tablespoons (½ stick) butter
2 tablespoons olive oil
2 large onions, finely chopped
2 large garlic cloves, finely chopped
2 tablespoons chopped fresh tarragon
    or 2 teaspoons dried
1 bay leaf
2 tablespoons all-purpose flour
2 cups chicken stock or vegetable broth

2 cups fresh or canned tomatoes,
    peeled, seeded, drained, and chopped
½ cup dry white wine
2 pounds mushrooms, sliced ¼ inch
    thick
½ ounce dried mushrooms, cut into
    small pieces
salt
freshly ground pepper
¼ cup chopped fresh parsley

1 In a saucepan heat 2 tablespoons butter and 1 tablespoon olive oil. Sauté onions until they begin to color, about 5 minutes. Add garlic, tarragon, and bay leaf and cook 2 more minutes.

2 Add flour and mix well. Cook until flour is blended, about 2 minutes. Add stock or broth, tomatoes, and wine and cook until all comes to a rapid boil. Reduce heat and simmer for 10 minutes. Remove from heat and set aside.

3 In a flameproof casserole with cover, heat remaining 2 tablespoons butter and 1 tablespoon oil. Add fresh and dried mushrooms and sauté over high heat for 3 minutes. Add tomato mixture, salt, and pepper, cover and cook for about 5 minutes. Stir in chopped parsley; taste and adjust seasoning. Serve hot.

Vegetable Casserole

SERVES 6

Eva Calogridis, born in Cyprus and the mother of a large family in New York, used to make the best vegetable casseroles of any neighbor and friend we knew. She used only fresh vegetables and herbs. See photo 4 following page 252.

½ cup olive oil
2 medium onions, sliced about ¼ inch thick
1 pound boiling potatoes, peeled, washed, dried, and sliced ¼ inch thick
6 small zucchini (about 1 × 6 inches), ends trimmed and sliced ½ inch thick
2 cups fresh tomatoes, cored, blanched, peeled, seeded, and cut into ½-inch cubes, or 2 cups canned plum tomatoes, drained and squeezed to remove seeds

2 bell peppers (1 green, 1 red), cored, seeds and membranes removed, and sliced ½ inch long
2 large garlic cloves, minced
1 teaspoon sugar
salt
freshly ground pepper
¼ cup chopped fresh parsley
1 heaping tablespoon chopped fresh fennel or 1 teaspoon fennel seed

1 Use 1 tablespoon olive oil to oil a 14 × 9 × 2-inch oval baking dish (one with a cover — if not, you can use foil) and arrange half of the onion slices on the bottom.

2 In a large bowl combine potatoes, zucchini, tomatoes, peppers, garlic, sugar, salt, pepper, half of the parsley, and the fennel. Mix well. Spoon this mixture onto onions; layer remaining onion slices on top.

3 Pour remaining oil overall and bake, covered, in preheated 350°F oven for 1½ hours, removing cover for the last 10 or 15 minutes of cooking. Pierce vegetables with a fork to check for doneness. Add remaining parsley before serving.

Cabbage, Carrots, and Chicken

SERVES 6

2 pounds cabbage
3 carrots, cooked and cut diagonally
   into 1-inch pieces
3 boned chicken breast halves, fat and
   skin removed
8 tablespoons (1 stick) butter (use some
   to butter casserole)

3 tablespoons all-purpose flour
2 cups chicken stock
1 tablespoon curry powder
salt and freshly ground pepper
½ cup fresh breadcrumbs

1 Remove any blemished outer leaves from cabbage. Halve cabbage and immerse in cool salted water for 30 minutes. Remove, shake out excess water and cut each half into 3 wedges. Fill a large saucepan ⅔ full with water, add some salt and bring to a boil. Add the cabbage, return water to boil and cook 6 minutes. Drain well. With a sharp knife, cut away core from each wedge and cut wedges into ½-inch slices. Transfer to buttered 1½- to 2-quart casserole. Add the carrots, tucking some under the cabbage.

2 Melt 2 tablespoons butter in a skillet and sauté the chicken breasts on each side until lightly browned, about 2 to 3 minutes per side. Remove and slice into ½ × 3-inch strips. Deglaze skillet with ½ cup chicken stock and pour every drop into casserole.

3 Heat the remaining 1½ cups chicken stock and add the curry. Simmer for 2 minutes; set aside. Melt 3 tablespoons butter in saucepan and add the flour. Whisk and cook for 2 minutes. Add the warm chicken stock, salt, and pepper and keep whisking until sauce thickens and is completely smooth. Pour evenly into casserole.

4 Sprinkle the crumbs overall, dot with remaining butter and bake, covered, for 25 minutes in preheated 350°F oven. Remove cover for 5 minutes additional baking.

Fresh Fennel Ratatouille

SERVES 6

2 small eggplants
salt
4 small zucchini
1/4 to 1/3 cup olive oil
2 medium onions, thinly sliced
3 garlic cloves, finely chopped
4 green frying peppers, cored, seeded, and cut into thin strips
1 large fennel bulb with leaves, thinly sliced

2 cups cored, blanched, peeled, and seeded fresh tomatoes cut into 1/2-inch cubes, or canned plum tomatoes put through a food mill
2 tablespoons chopped fresh dill or 1 teaspoon dried dillweed
leaves from 6 fresh parsley sprigs, finely chopped
salt and freshly ground pepper

1 Wash and dry eggplants. Discard ends. Do not peel. Cut into thin slices, salt lightly, and place in a colander. Wash and dry zucchini. Discard the ends. Cut into thin slices, salt lightly, and add to the eggplant slices. Allow vegetables to drain for about 30 minutes.

2 Dry vegetable slices with a paper towel. Heat a small amount of the oil in a large skillet and sauté eggplant slices in small batches; don't worry if they are lightly scorched. Transfer to paper toweling to drain. Add the zucchini slices and sauté, adding a little more oil as necessary during (don't overdo). Set zucchini on paper toweling to drain. Add a little more oil to same skillet and sauté the onions and garlic for about 5 minutes; do not burn garlic. Add the peppers, fennel, tomatoes, dill, and parsley. Cook for 2 minutes and remove from heat.

3 Arrange a layer of eggplant slices and then a layer of zucchini slices in a covered 2½-quart casserole. Spoon some of the tomato mixture over the slices. Add salt and pepper. Repeat the layers of eggplant and zucchini. Top with remaining tomato mixture. Season with salt and pepper. Cover and bake in preheated 350°F oven for about 1 hour.

Pepper, Potato, and Tomato Stew

SERVES 6

Tasty and easy to prepare.

6 tablespoons olive oil
1 sweet Italian or similar sausage, cut
  into ¼-inch slices
2 garlic cloves, finely chopped
4 cups cored, blanched, peeled, seeded,
  and coarsely chopped fresh
  tomatoes, or canned tomatoes put
  through a food mill
salt

freshly ground pepper
¼ cup finely chopped fresh basil
4 medium boiling potatoes, cut into
  ½-inch cubes
2 pounds green or red frying peppers
  (or a mixture of both), cored, seeded,
  and quartered
2 medium onions, sliced
⅓ cup dry red wine (optional)

1 Heat 1 tablespoon olive oil in a large saucepan, add the sausage, and brown on all sides for 5 minutes. Add garlic and sauté for 1 minute. Add tomatoes, salt, pepper, and basil and cook over medium heat for 10 minutes. Add potatoes and cook an additional 20 minutes.

2 Heat 5 tablespoons oil in another large saucepan, add the peppers and sauté for 10 minutes. Add onions and cook 5 minutes; the vegetables should be firm.

3 Add the peppers and onions to the tomato mixture and toss well. Cover and cook an additional 20 minutes. Taste and adjust the seasonings. Uncover and add the red wine for the last 5 minutes of cooking, if you wish.

A Vegetable Casserole with Onions, Celery, Peppers, Tomatoes, Eggplant, and Eggs

SERVES 6 TO 8

1 large or 2 small eggplants
2 tablespoons salt
2 small to medium zucchini
8 tablespoons (1 stick) butter
2 medium onions, coarsely chopped
  (about 1½ cups)
2 garlic cloves, finely chopped
3 stalks celery with leaves (strings
  removed), coarsely chopped (about
  1 cup)
2 green frying peppers, cored, seeded,
  and coarsely chopped

4 large tomatoes, cored, blanched,
  peeled, seeded, and cubed (about
  2 cups), or 2 cups canned plum
  tomatoes put through a food mill
¼ cup chopped fresh basil or
  1 tablespoon dried
2 tablespoons chopped fresh thyme or
  1 teaspoon dried
freshly ground pepper
1½ cups fresh coarse breadcrumbs
2 tablespoons oil
6 to 8 eggs

1 Wash and dry the eggplant(s). Cut off and discard the ends, but do not peel. Cut eggplant into ¾-inch cubes to make about 5 cups. Place the eggplant cubes in a colander and sprinkle with salt.

2 Wash and dry the zucchini. Cut them in quarters lengthwise, but do not peel. Scoop out the seedy central pulp (if the zucchini are very small, this won't be necessary), and cut the zucchini quarters into ¾-inch cubes to make about 4 cups. Add the zucchini cubes to the eggplant in the colander, toss them together, and allow them to drain for 1 hour.

3 Melt 4 tablespoons butter in a large saucepan and cook the onions for 5 minutes, or until softened. Add the garlic and cook 2 more minutes. Add the celery, peppers, eggplant, zucchini, tomatoes, basil, thyme, and pepper. Stir and cook over high heat for 5 minutes.

4 Use 2 tablespoons butter to grease an 8 × 12 × 2-inch baking dish or similar-size casserole with a cover. Sprinkle bottom of the dish with ½ cup breadcrumbs. Fill the baking dish with the vegetable mixture. Top with the remaining 1 cup breadcrumbs and dot with the remaining 2 tablespoons butter and the oil. Bake, covered, in preheated 400°F oven for 30 minutes or until vegetables are cooked through and bubbling; 10 minutes before end of baking time, remove from oven and break eggs into baking dish, spacing them as evenly as you can. Return to oven and continue cooking until eggs are set and vegetables are tender.

Tomato, Bread, and Egg Casserole

SERVES 6

This makes a wonderful brunch dish. Serve with crisp bacon and a salad.

1 loaf (1 pound) homemade-type white bread
8 tablespoons (1 stick) butter
3 cups canned plum tomatoes (one 28-ounce can), including liquid, put through a food mill
1 cup grated carrot
1 cup grated celery
6 tablespoons firmly packed brown sugar
¼ cup finely chopped fresh basil or 1 teaspoon dried
salt
freshly ground pepper
6 eggs

1 Slice bread ½ inch thick and remove crusts. Cut into ½-inch cubes. Melt butter in a large skillet, add bread cubes, and cook until edges brown. Remove from heat.

2 Combine tomatoes, carrot, celery, brown sugar, basil, salt, and pepper in a saucepan. Bring mixture to a boil and remove from heat. Taste and adjust seasoning.

3 Arrange bread in a 2-quart casserole and pour tomato mixture overall. Bake in preheated 375°F oven for 15 minutes. Remove from oven and with the back of a tablespoon make evenly spaced indentations to hold eggs on top of mixture. Break an egg into each hollow and continue to bake for 15 minutes or until eggs are set. Season with more pepper and serve hot with lots of fresh greens and a cold sliced beet salad.

Red Cabbage and Chestnuts, Sweet and Sour

SERVES 6

Red cabbage is especially tasty prepared this way. It tastes even better reheated the next day. See photo 2 following page 60.

2 pounds red cabbage
12 spareribs
⅔ cup sugar
⅓ cup water
¼ cup red wine vinegar
½ teaspoon ground cumin

½ teaspoon caraway seed
½ cup water
salt
freshly ground pepper
1 cup cooked whole chestnuts, peeled

1 In a large saucepan or stockpot bring salted water to a boil. Meanwhile, shred cabbage in a food processor or slice very thinly by hand. Boil cabbage for 12 minutes. Drain and set aside.

2 Arrange spareribs at the bottom of a large saucepan, making 2 or 3 layers as necessary. Cover with water, bring to a boil, lower heat, and simmer for 15 minutes. Drain and dry ribs; broil until they begin to brown. Set aside.

3 Combine sugar and ⅓ cup water in flameproof 2½- to 3-quart casserole with a cover. Stir constantly over high heat until sugar dissolves and begins to caramelize, about 7 minutes; watch carefully to avoid burning. Add vinegar, cumin, and caraway and cook for 3 to 4 minutes more.

4 Preheat oven to 375°F. Transfer the drained cabbage to the casserole and toss lightly. Arrange spareribs on top and add chestnuts to the casserole. Add water, cover casserole and bake for 50 minutes, or until cabbage is done. Salt and pepper to taste and serve hot.

Wild Rice and Vegetable Casserole

SERVES 6

1 cup wild rice
2 cups chicken stock or vegetable broth
5 tablespoons unsalted butter
1 red bell pepper, cored, seeded, and finely chopped (about 1 cup)
1½ cups finely chopped celery (about 4 stalks)
1 cup finely chopped onion
1 cup thinly sliced mushrooms

3 tablespoons all-purpose flour
1 cup milk (or additional chicken stock or vegetable broth)
1 cup light cream (or ½ cup stock or broth and ½ cup light cream)
salt
freshly grated nutmeg
freshly ground pepper
½ cup slivered toasted almonds

1 Rinse the rice twice in cold water to remove any foreign particles; drain. Bring 2 cups stock or broth to rapid boil in heavy saucepan. Add the rice, lower the heat, cover tightly, and simmer for 45 to 50 minutes, or until the grains are tender and the broth is absorbed.

2 Melt 2 tablespoons butter in a large saucepan. Add the pepper, celery, and onion and sauté for 4 minutes. Add the mushrooms and cook an additional 2 minutes. Set aside.

3 Preheat the oven to 400°F. Melt remaining 3 tablespoons butter in a saucepan and add the flour. Remove from heat immediately and mix together thoroughly. Whisk in the milk and cream, return to moderate heat, and bring to a boil, whisking constantly. When sauce is thick and smooth, lower the heat and simmer for 2 to 3 minutes. Stir in the salt and nutmeg to taste.

4 Add the sauce to the rice mixture, season with salt and pepper, and mix well. Transfer to a 1½-quart casserole and sprinkle with almonds. Cover and bake for 30 minutes, then remove cover and bake an additional 10 minutes. You may serve this straight from the casserole, or spoon onto leaves of red leaf lettuce on individual serving plates.

Bean and Vegetable Casserole

SERVES 4 TO 6

1 cup dried navy or pea beans
4 cups water
1 tablespoon oil
1 pound boneless leg of lamb, trimmed of fat and cut into 1-inch pieces
2 tablespoons butter
6 small whole boiling white onions
1 medium leek (including tender green parts), halved lengthwise, washed thoroughly, and cut into ½-inch slices
3 carrots, peeled and cut into 2-inch pieces
2 garlic cloves, finely chopped

1 teaspoon finely chopped fresh rosemary or ½ teaspoon dried, crumbled
1 teaspoon finely chopped fresh thyme or ½ teaspoon dried
1½ cups beef stock
1 cup canned plum tomatoes, put through a food mill
2 strips (4 × 1 inches each) orange zest
3 cups turnips, peeled and cut into 1-inch pieces
salt and freshly ground pepper

1 In a heavy saucepan combine beans and 2 cups water. Bring to a rapid boil, then remove from heat, cover tightly, and let the beans stand for 1 hour. Add 2 more cups water to the beans and bring to rapid boil over medium-high heat. Reduce the heat, cover tightly, and simmer for 1 hour or until beans are firm but tender. Drain well.

2 Heat the oil in a large flameproof casserole. Add the lamb pieces and brown on all sides; this will take about 15 minutes. Transfer the lamb to a bowl. Melt the butter in the same casserole. Add the onions, leek, carrots, and garlic and sauté for 5 minutes. Add the rosemary and thyme. Return the lamb to the vegetables and add beef stock, tomatoes, and orange zest. Cover and simmer for 1½ hours, or until the vegetables and lamb are *almost* tender. Add the beans to the casserole. Cover and cook 30 minutes. Add the turnips and cook an additional 10 minutes or until lamb and vegetables are tender. Season to taste with salt and pepper and serve hot.

Vegetable Tamale Pie

SERVES 6 TO 8

See photo 2 following page 140.

8 slices bacon
1 cup finely chopped onion
1 medium-size red bell pepper, cored,
  seeded, and coarsely chopped
3 garlic cloves, finely chopped
2 cups canned tomatoes, seeded and
  chopped
1½ cups whole kernel corn, fresh,
  frozen, or canned

2 jalapeño peppers, finely chopped
2 tablespoons chili powder
1 teaspoon ground cumin
1 teaspoon ground coriander
salt
2 cups yellow cornmeal
5 cups beef stock
1 tablespoon vegetable oil
2 tablespoons butter

1 In a large saucepan cook the bacon until crisp. Drain on paper towels and set aside. Discard all but 2 tablespoons bacon fat from saucepan. Add onion, red pepper, and garlic and sauté about 2 minutes; do not let the vegetables brown. Add the tomatoes, corn, jalapeño peppers, chili powder, cumin, coriander, and salt to taste. Mix well and cook over medium-high heat for 5 minutes. Set aside.

2 Preheat oven to 400°F. In a heavy large saucepan combine cornmeal, salt to taste, beef stock, and the vegetable oil. Bring to boil, lower the heat, and cook until thickened, whisking constantly. Let the cornmeal mush cool slightly (do not let it get too cold; it should be thick, but easy to spread in the baking pan).

3 Butter a deep 7½ × 10½ × 2-inch baking dish. Spread half of the cornmeal mixture on the bottom and sides. Add the vegetable filling and crumble the bacon on top. Add the remaining cornmeal and smooth it over. Dot butter overall.

4 Bake for 45 to 50 minutes or until the top is brown. Before serving, garnish top with uncooked red bell pepper.

10

SOUFFLÉS AND OMELETS

Vegetables are excellent additions to one of the most appealing culinary treats: the soufflé, golden, light as a feather, and beautiful to look at. It may be true that making soufflés is like walking a tightrope; both create a rather intense fear of falling. But you will succeed if you understand and follow certain soufflé-making basics.

Traditionally, a soufflé consists of a white sauce enriched with milk or cream and egg yolks, flavored with one or more other ingredients (vegetables, cheese, meat, or fish, for example), and lightened with beaten egg whites. The moisture in the soufflé turns to steam in the hot oven and puffs up the soufflé — in other words, the small air bubbles in the egg whites expand during baking and inflate the mixture.

Nouvelle cuisine enthusiasts have adapted the traditional soufflé procedure by eliminating the cream sauce and milk and binding the mixture with ricotta or cream cheese instead. Both these and the traditional types are included in this chapter.

To allay your fears about soufflés remember a few simple rules: (a) liberally butter the dish to help the soufflé move up the baking container; (b) when combining the butter and flour to make the sauce, cook them together for 2 or 3 minutes to cook the flour *before* adding milk or other liquid — this removes any floury taste; (c) separate eggs carefully and whisk or beat the egg whites to a massive foam before adding to other ingredients. Egg whites should make *soft*, not stiff peaks. Whisk or beat egg whites *just before* baking or they will begin to deflate. Fold them in gently. Don't worry if you see a few white streaks, since overmixing will also deflate egg whites. (d) Do not fill soufflé dish to the brim — except when making individual ones — or they will spill over. About ⅔ to ¾ full is right. Whatever the size of the soufflé, run your thumb around the edge of the mixture to make a rather deep groove; this helps soufflé rise in the center and "caps" it. (e) It's usually easier to make individual soufflés rather than one large one. They take only about half the time, are more sure of success, and they can be eaten right out of the dish. Two different individual soufflés plus a salad make a terrific meal.

Shallots or green onions will give life to a soufflé, as will artichokes, celeriac or fresh green peas. For richness and subtlety, soufflés and omelets can't be beat.

Opposite: Fresh Basil and Tomato Soup (page 226).

Shallot and Parsley Soufflé

SERVES 6

10 tablespoons (1¼ sticks) butter
10 shallots, finely chopped (about 1 cup)
6 tablespoons all-purpose flour
1¼ cups chicken stock or vegetable
   broth, heated
salt
freshly ground pepper

½ cup chopped fresh parsley, preferably
   flat-leaf
1¼ cups shredded Gruyère or Swiss
   cheese
6 egg yolks, beaten
7 egg whites

1 Melt 4 tablespoons butter in a large skillet. Add shallots and sauté until they begin to color. Remove from heat and set aside.

2 Melt remaining butter in a saucepan. When it begins to bubble, add flour and whisk constantly for 2 to 3 minutes; do not let flour brown. Add stock or broth and continue whisking and cooking until mixture boils and thickens. Add salt and season liberally with pepper. Add shallots, parsley, cheese, and egg yolks and cook until well blended and cheese has completely melted. Remove from heat and cool.

3 Beat egg whites until they form soft peaks. Add ⅓ of beaten whites to shallot mixture and fold in lightly and carefully. Repeat with next third, then with remaining whites.

4 Turn mixture into a generously buttered 2-quart soufflé dish. Run your thumb around edge to make a groove. Bake in preheated 375°F oven for 45 minutes. Soufflé should be browned and fairly high. Serve right away.

Opposite: Whole Savoy Cabbage with
Four Stuffings (page 106).

Zucchini Soufflé with Lemon

❦

SERVES 4

2 cups peeled and coarsely grated
* zucchini (about 2 medium)*
salt
4 tablespoons (½ stick) unsalted butter
2 tablespoons finely chopped onion
2 tablespoons finely chopped shallot
¼ cup all-purpose flour
½ cup milk
½ cup light cream

¼ cup Brie cheese cut into ¼-inch cubes
4 egg yolks, beaten
1 tablespoon fresh lemon juice
1 tablespoon finely chopped or grated
* lemon zest*
freshly ground pepper
4 egg whites
1 cup freshly grated Parmesan cheese

1 Put the zucchini in a colander and set it over a bowl. Add 1 teaspoon salt and let stand for 30 minutes. With your hands, squeeze as much moisture as you can from the zucchini.

2 Melt butter in a large saucepan over moderate heat without browning it. Add onion and shallot and sauté for 2 minutes; do not brown. Lower the heat, add the flour and stir together thoroughly for 2 to 3 minutes. Add the milk and cream and keep stirring constantly until the sauce boils and is thickened and smooth (this will take about 5 minutes). Add the Brie and keep stirring until melted and smooth. Remove from heat.

3 Add the zucchini, egg yolks, lemon juice, lemon zest, and salt and pepper to the cheese mixture and blend well.

4 Beat the egg whites to soft peaks and fold carefully into the zucchini mixture.

5 Spoon into a buttered 8- or 9-inch soufflé dish and bake in a preheated 350°F oven for 35 to 40 minutes, or until soufflé is risen and has a beautiful golden color. Serve immediately, passing the Parmesan cheese separately.

❦

Tomato-Basil Soufflé

MAKES 5 MEDIUM OR 8 SMALL INDIVIDUAL SOUFFLÉS

2 tablespoons olive oil
2 garlic cloves, finely chopped
2 cups drained canned plum tomatoes
1 tablespoon sugar
salt
freshly ground pepper

¼ cup finely chopped fresh basil or
   1 teaspoon dried
½ cup skim-milk ricotta
8 eggs, separated
Basil Cream Sauce (page 263)

1 Butter five 1¼-cup or eight ¾-cup individual soufflé dishes. Arrange on a baking sheet and refrigerate.

2 Heat olive oil in a skillet, add garlic, and sauté 1 minute. Add tomatoes and sugar and cook uncovered for 25 minutes. Salt and pepper to taste and puree in food mill (do not use food processor, as it will grind bitter tomato seeds into puree). You should have 1½ cups puree; if you have more, cook down further.

3 Combine tomato puree, basil, and ricotta in food processor or whisk thoroughly by hand. Taste and adjust seasoning. Transfer puree to a bowl and whisk in egg yolks.

4 Beat egg whites to soft peaks. Fold about ⅓ of whites into puree, then fold in remaining whites; do not overfold. Spoon soufflé mixture into prepared dishes, filling to the rim and running your thumb around outer edge to make a groove. Be sure no mixture is on rim of baking dish, as it may prevent soufflé from rising.

5 Bake for 12 minutes in preheated 425°F oven. Immediately transfer each soufflé to a serving plate. With a spoon make a break in the top of each soufflé and place 1 or 2 tablespoons Basil Cream Sauce in the opening. Serve right away.

Broccoli Ricotta Soufflé

SERVES 4

3 tablespoons unsalted butter
2 tablespoons olive oil
½ cup finely chopped onion
1 cup finely chopped cooked broccoli
1 pound skim-milk ricotta
3 large eggs, lightly beaten

½ cup freshly grated Parmesan cheese
salt
freshly ground pepper
4 egg whites
¼ cup breadcrumbs

1 Heat the butter and oil in a skillet, add onion and sauté over moderate heat, stirring, until soft. Stir in broccoli and cook 2 minutes longer. Transfer the mixture to a large bowl and add the ricotta, whole eggs, Parmesan, and salt and pepper to taste. Mix well.

2 Beat the egg whites in an electric mixer until they hold soft peaks. Fold ⅓ of the whites into the ricotta mixture, then fold in the remaining whites gently but thoroughly.

3 Butter a 1½-quart soufflé dish and sprinkle with crumbs, shaking out any excess. Transfer the broccoli mixture to the soufflé dish, running your thumb around edge to make a groove. Bake in preheated 375°F oven for 35 to 40 minutes, or until puffed and golden brown. Serve immediately.

Individual Fiddlehead Soufflés

SERVES 6

1¾ pounds fresh fiddleheads
4 cups water
½ cup ricotta
freshly grated nutmeg
salt

freshly ground pepper
8 eggs, separated, at room temperature
3 tablespoons freshly grated Parmesan
  or mild Cheddar cheese
Sauce Bâtarde (page 255)

1 Butter six 4½ × 2½-inch baking cups and chill for 30 minutes.

2 To clean fiddleheads, snap off the crisp bright green fiddlehead top from the ostrich fern, leaving 2 inches of the stem attached. Rub off the dry brown casings. Let the fiddleheads soak in a large bowl of cold water, changing the water about 3 times to remove any grit or casing particles; drain. Fiddleheads can be kept in refrigerator, covered, up to 1 week.

3 Preheat the oven to 425°F. In a saucepan bring water to a rapid boil. Add the fiddleheads and return to boil. Lower the heat and simmer the fiddleheads for 12 to 15 minutes or until tender.

4 In a food processor combine the fiddleheads, ricotta, nutmeg, and salt and pepper to taste and puree (there should be 3 cups). Transfer the mixture to a large bowl, add the yolks, and blend well with a wire whisk.

5 Beat egg whites until soft peaks form. Fold about ⅓ of whites into the fiddlehead mixture. Fold in remaining whites carefully; do not overfold.

6 Fill the cups to the rim and arrange on a baking sheet. Run your thumb around the edge of each cup to make a groove. Be sure no mixture is on rim of dish, as it may prevent soufflé from rising. Bake for 12 to 15 minutes. Serve immediately with sauce.

Celery Soufflé with St. André Cheese

SERVES 8

16 (1 × ¼ inch each) pieces St. André
  cheese (about 8 ounces), or Boursault
4 cups thinly sliced celery with tender
  green leaves
1 onion, sliced

¾ cup skim-milk ricotta
1 teaspoon celery seed
salt and freshly ground pepper
8 eggs, separated
Tarragon Cream Sauce (page 264)

1 Butter eight 1-cup individual soufflé dishes. Put 2 pieces of cheese in the bottom of each dish, arrange on baking sheet and refrigerate.

2 Cook celery and onion in boiling salted water until tender, about 8 minutes. Drain well and pat dry. Let cool. Puree celery and onion in food processor; it should measure 2 full cups. Transfer to a fine strainer and drain for 10 minutes or so. Add ricotta, celery seed, and salt and pepper to taste and blend. Transfer puree to a bowl and whisk in egg yolks.

3 Beat egg whites to soft peaks. Fold about ⅓ of whites into puree, then fold in remaining whites; do not overfold. Spoon soufflé mixture into individual dishes, filling to the rim and running your thumb around edge to make a groove. Be sure no mixture is on rim of baking dish, as it may prevent soufflé from rising. Bake for 12 minutes in preheated 425°F oven. Immediately transfer each soufflé to a serving plate. With a spoon make a break in the top of each soufflé and place 1 or 2 tablespoons Tarragon Cream Sauce in the opening. Serve right away.

Green Pea Soufflé with Mint

MAKES 5 MEDIUM OR 8 SMALL INDIVIDUAL SOUFFLÉS

*1¼ pounds shelled fresh green peas or
two 10-ounce packages frozen peas
2 tablespoons finely chopped fresh
mint or 1 tablespoon dried
4 green onions, finely chopped*

*½ cup skim-milk ricotta
salt
freshly ground pepper
8 eggs, separated
5 tablespoons butter, softened*

1 Butter five 1¼-cup or eight ¾-cup individual soufflé dishes. Arrange on a baking sheet and refrigerate.

2 Cook peas in boiling salted water until tender. Drain well and pat dry. Puree with mint in food processor or blender (there will be about 2 cups). Transfer to a large mixing bowl and add green onions, ricotta, salt, and pepper. Mix well. Whisk in egg yolks.

3 Beat egg whites to soft peaks. Fold about ⅓ of whites into puree, then fold in remaining whites; do not overfold. Spoon soufflé mixture into prepared dishes, filling to the rim and running your thumb around edge to make a groove. Be sure no mixture is on rim of baking dish, as it may prevent soufflé from rising.

4 Bake for 12 minutes in preheated 425°F oven. Immediately transfer each soufflé to a serving plate. With a spoon make a break in the top of each soufflé and place a dollop of soft butter in the opening.

Swiss Chard and Potato Pie

SERVES 4

This simple, wonderful, and satisfying dish is a specialty of Loretta DiFranco, who was born and raised in Pittsburgh. She serves it with crusty Italian or French bread and thick slices of really ripe tomato.

1 bunch fresh Swiss chard (about
   1 pound)
3 quarts water
2 tablespoons butter
¼ cup olive or vegetable oil
4 large shallots, minced

2 garlic cloves, minced
4 boiling potatoes, peeled and thinly
   sliced
salt
freshly ground pepper

1 Discard large Swiss chard leaves. Wash the greens carefully and peel the white stems with a vegetable peeler. Cut stems into 1-inch pieces and leaves into 3-inch pieces.

2 Boil 3 quarts water in a large pot. Add the Swiss chard and return to boil. Lower heat and cook the chard for 4 to 5 minutes; do not overcook. Drain and rinse under cold water; set aside (there should be about 3 cups Swiss chard).

3 Heat butter and oil in a 10-inch skillet. Add the shallots and garlic and sauté until light brown.

4 Add half of potatoes and chard; season with salt and pepper. Add the remaining potatoes and chard and salt and pepper liberally. Cover the skillet and cook over medium to high heat for 10 to 12 minutes, or until bottom of pie is golden brown.

5 Invert the pie onto a plate and slide it back into the skillet (you may need to add a little more oil to the skillet for this step). Cook uncovered for 10 minutes or until bottom is golden brown. Serve immediately.

Oven Zucchini Omelet

SERVES 4 TO 5

1 pound zucchini, ends trimmed (do
   not peel), coarsely grated
salt
4 eggs, beaten
1 medium onion, coarsely chopped
1 red bell pepper or 1 large green or
   red frying pepper, cored, seeded,
   and diced

1 garlic clove, finely chopped
2 tablespoons chopped fresh parsley
3 or 4 green onions (including tender
   green parts), chopped
salt
freshly ground pepper
¼ cup grated pecorino Romano cheese

1 Set zucchini in a colander over a bowl and sprinkle with salt. Let the zucchini drain for 30 minutes.

2 Squeeze out all moisture from zucchini with hands or the back of a wooden spoon.

3 In a large bowl combine the zucchini, eggs, onion, diced pepper, garlic, parsley, green onions, salt, pepper, and cheese. Mix well.

4 Pour into an oiled 9-inch ceramic quiche dish or pie plate and bake in preheated 350°F oven for 40 to 45 minutes or until nicely puffed.

5 Let rest for 3 or 4 minutes, then serve the zucchini omelet directly from the dish. It may also be served cold.

Yellow Squash and Onion Omelet

SERVES 4

1 pound small unpeeled yellow squash
¼ cup vegetable oil
2 medium onions, finely chopped
1 red bell pepper, cored, seeded, and
  chopped

6 eggs, room temperature
1 teaspoon sugar
1 teaspoon turmeric
salt
freshly ground pepper

1 Wash and dry squash. Cut off ends and slice thinly. Cook the squash in 2 inches of water for 2 to 3 minutes or until tender. Drain and set aside.

2 Heat the oil in an 8- to 10-inch skillet. Add the squash, onions, and pepper and sauté until lightly browned.

3 Combine eggs, sugar, turmeric, salt, and pepper in a bowl and beat well. Pour the egg mixture into the skillet and cover. Cook over medium-high heat until the omelet is set on the bottom, about 3 minutes. Invert omelet onto a 12-inch plate. Pour off any oil remaining in skillet. Slip omelet back into skillet and cook for 2 to 3 minutes longer or until second side is nicely browned. Transfer omelet to a serving platter or serve directly from the skillet.

11

MAIN COURSE SALADS

It's always fun to leave New York on a late Friday afternoon in the summer to drive to the high-ceilinged, cool rooms of our Greek Revival house in Dutchess County. With a basket of fresh figs and a wedge of pecorino or St. André cheese having just reached room temperature as we put the key through the kitchen door, supper is almost ready. There's a quick walk to the garden to harvest fresh lettuces, vegetables, and herbs — perhaps to whip up lettuce hearts with garlic butter or tomato slices with basil and cream. And the chilled bottle of Sauvignon Blanc is only a step away.

The kitchen table is set — it sits alongside two large windows overlooking a little sea of day lilies, with a menagerie of ceramic animals on the inside sill. They look as if they, too, can hardly wait to nibble at the salad greens.

It has often been said that good cooking is honest, simple, and sincere. However true this may be, at no time should it imply that turning out fine food can be done in no time and with no trouble. This is especially true in dealing with salads. Yes, a good salad is honest, simple, and sincere; but it *does* take some effort, and its preparation — including the shopping for ingredients — should be thought of as a labor of love. Always consider what's in season. (We've written elsewhere about tasteless, pale pink "hothouse" tomatoes, overgrown string beans, aged broccoli flowerets.) Nowhere is the freshness of ingredients more important than in a salad, and especially when it is intended to be the main course.

If ever there was a fault in handling salad ingredients (even in some of the better restaurants), it is in leaving them wet. Oil and water simply won't mix, and the moisture on salad greens and vegetables weakens the dressing to near oblivion. By all means, *dry* salad ingredients before tossing them with dressing. One doesn't need a salad spinner or similar piece of equipment, although they do their work well (in fact, they provide the easiest way to dry salad greens). You can instead use clean linen or cotton towels to pat the greens dry lightly and thoroughly. You will be rewarded with much better-tasting salads.

Salads offer an infinite variety of compositions. In addition to a number of main-dish recipes, we include single-vegetable salads of which two, three, or four can be nicely arranged on a plate and accompanied by some cheese, bread, a taste of spicy sausage, a variety of olives, and perhaps a few slices of cured meats to make an ideal meal. Greens for salads are plentiful, and we can't think of a single vegetable which couldn't find an interesting and tasty place in salad. Can you?

Potato Salad with Smoked Salmon

SERVES 6 TO 8

So simple, and one of the most delicious preparations in this book. It uses very little salmon, but the taste is there. See photo 4 following page 60.

3 pounds small new red potatoes
¼ cup Dijon mustard
¼ cup sugar
¼ cup white wine vinegar
½ cup finely chopped fresh dill or
  2 teaspoons dried dillweed or dill seed

salt
freshly ground pepper
¾ cup vegetable, corn, or peanut oil
4 ounces smoked salmon, sliced and
  cut into ½-inch pieces

1 Scrub potatoes but do not peel. Put them in a saucepan and add water to cover. Bring to boil and simmer until tender, about 20 minutes. Drain potatoes and pat dry. Cut them into quarters and place in a large mixing bowl.

2 In a smaller mixing bowl or in food processor, combine mustard, sugar, vinegar, dill, and salt and pepper to taste. Blend thoroughly. (If mixing by hand, whisk in the oil a little at a time until all oil is blended. If using processor, pour oil through feed tube a little at a time as if making mayonnaise.) If you want a thinner sauce, blend in 1 to 2 tablespoons warm water.

3 Pour sauce over the potatoes and mix well but carefully in order not to break up potatoes. Add salmon and toss lightly. May be served warm or cold.

Vegetable Salad à la Russe

SERVES 8

A Russian salad is a mixture of cooked vegetables, diced and masked with dressing. There are a hundred or more versions of this recipe. Tender uncooked celery hearts add a beautiful note to any salad. In this recipe they do exactly that, especially with the addition of our pale green mayonnaise. See photo 1 opposite page 140.

1 pound boiling potatoes, cubed
8 ounces turnips, cubed
1 pound carrots, sliced diagonally
  (about 2 cups)
1 pound green beans, ends trimmed,
  cut diagonally into 1-inch lengths
8 ounces snow peas, ends trimmed, cut
  diagonally into 1-inch lengths
1 cup shelled fresh or frozen green peas
1 cup thinly sliced raw celery heart
  with leaves
juice of 1 lemon
salt
freshly ground pepper
6 green onion leaves, washed and
  blanched until flexible
1 beet, cooked and thinly sliced
1 hard-cooked egg, thinly sliced
3 black olives, pitted and cut into
  ¼-inch slices

3 anchovies, cut lengthwise to make
  6 strips
1 green onion (white part only) cut
  into ¼-inch slices
1 cup finely chopped fresh parsley

PALE GREEN MAYONNAISE
½ cup coarsely chopped watercress
  leaves
½ cup coarsely chopped fresh parsley
½ cup coarsely chopped young spinach
  leaves
¼ cup fresh or frozen green peas,
  cooked until tender and cooled
¼ cup coarsely chopped fresh chives
1 tablespoon fresh lemon juice
2 cups homemade Mayonnaise
  (page 261)
salt
¼ teaspoon white pepper

1 Combine all ingredients for the mayonnaise in food processor fitted with the steel knife and process until the mixture is smooth, about 1 minute. The mayonnaise will be more flavorful if it is made ahead and refrigerated for several hours before mixing with salad.

2 Bring large pot of salted water to boil. In turn, cook potatoes, turnips, carrots, green beans, snow peas, and green peas, removing each with slotted spoon or strainer as it is cooked. Do not overcook the vegetables. Drain each vegetable and run under cool water.

3 Put all the cooked vegetables and the celery into a large mixing bowl and add the lemon juice, green mayonnaise, and salt and pepper to taste. Mix well. Refrigerate for 30 minutes to firm up salad. Transfer mixture to a large serving platter and shape it in the form of a large half Easter egg or melon mold.

4 Decorate the salad as follows: arrange the blanched green onion leaves in the form of flower stems atop salad.

5 Place a circle of beet at the end of each stalk. On top of each beet place an egg slice, and on top of that a slice of olive (the idea is for each succeeding layer to be smaller than the previous one).

6 Coil each anchovy strip to make a circle about ¾ to 1 inch in diameter. Place at stem ends to serve as bloom bases. Add a slice of green onion on top of each anchovy coil. Sprinkle with parsley.

Cauliflower Cornucopia

SERVES 8

Vegetables cooked in a bamboo steamer are delicious. Simply place steamer in a wok and add water to the bottom of the wok until steamer sits about 1 inch above water line. Remove steamer, arrange vegetables in it, bring water to a boil, replace steamer in wok, cover, and time steaming as in recipe. A bamboo steamer can also be used with a skillet of the same diameter as the steamer. Again, leave 1 inch space between the water line and the bottom of the steamer. Steam over medium to high heat, never losing the boil.

To create the intended effect, buy a large cauliflower head whose outer leaves are also large. Do not buy an overly trimmed head, usually wrapped in cellophane, as once the flowerets are removed the shell will not be large enough to hold the vegetables. See photo 1 following page 28.

1 large cauliflower (at least 3 pounds), with green leaves attached
juice of 1 lemon
1 tablespoon salt
3 to 4 carrots, sliced diagonally less than ¼ inch thick (2 cups)
2 cups whole Brussels sprouts, trimmed
10 large red radishes, stemmed and thinly sliced
⅔ cup oil-cured black olives, pitted (see note)
½ cup green onion, sliced diagonally ¼ inch thick

1 cup fresh uncooked snow peas, ends trimmed, halved crosswise
⅓ cup finely chopped fresh parsley

DRESSING
(makes about 1 cup)
2 garlic cloves, halved
¼ cup white wine vinegar
⅔ cup olive oil
2 teaspoons salt
freshly ground pepper
2 tablespoons Dijon mustard
1 tablespoon chopped fresh oregano or 1 teaspoon dried

1 For dressing, combine all ingredients and let stand overnight or longer. Discard garlic.

2 Combine cauliflower head, lemon juice, and salt in large pan or bowl and cover with water. Let stand 1 hour. Drain cauliflower and carefully cut away flowerets in about 1½-inch pieces. Remove 2 cups flowerets and reserve for another use. Keep leaves intact so cauliflower maintains its shape. Cut away as much core as possible, snip away fading leaf portions, and slice bottom end of core so cauliflower shell will sit upright. Immerse shell in ice water, cover, and set in refrigerator.

3 Steam carrot slices in a covered steamer basket over boiling water until tender, about 7 minutes. Drain and run under cold water. Drain again and dry in kitchen toweling. Set aside.

4 Steam Brussels sprouts in a covered steamer basket over boiling water until tender, about 6 to 8 minutes depending on size. Drain and run under cold water. Drain again and dry in kitchen toweling. Set aside.

5 Steam cauliflower flowerets in a covered steamer basket over boiling water until tender, about 7 minutes. Drain and run under cold water. Drain again and dry in kitchen toweling. Combine with radishes, carrots, Brussels sprouts, olives, green onion, snow peas, parsley, and dressing. Cover and refrigerate until 1 or 2 hours before serving (this can stay in refrigerator, covered, for several days). If prepared a day or more in advance, do not add radish slices until 1 to 2 hours before serving to avoid discoloration of radish.

6 Fill cauliflower shell with vegetable mixture. Serve at room temperature.

NOTE
This cornucopia is tastiest with the cured olives that are found in many delicatessens and specialty shops. If you can't get them, use canned pitted olives.

Salad of Chinese Cabbage

SERVES 6

5 cups finely chopped Chinese cabbage
4 small zucchini, ends trimmed (do
  not peel)
1 small cucumber, ends trimmed,
  partially peeled
1 cup diced water chestnuts
1 large green bell pepper, cored and
  seeded
1 large red bell pepper, cored and seeded
3 medium-size purple onions, thinly
  sliced in rings
¾ cup finely chopped fresh parsley

6 thin strips red bell pepper
6 thin strips green bell pepper

DRESSING
(makes about 1 cup)
2 garlic cloves, cut into 4 or 5 pieces
¼ cup white wine vinegar
¾ cup olive or vegetable oil
2 teaspoons Dijon mustard
1 teaspoon salt
freshly ground pepper

1 Put garlic pieces for dressing along with vinegar in a bowl and let stand for 1 hour or longer.

2 Press the garlic pieces against the side of the bowl with the back of a wooden spoon. Discard garlic. Add the oil, mustard, salt, and pepper and mix until all is blended.

3 Cut the cabbage, zucchini, cucumber, water chestnuts, and red and green peppers into ½-inch cubes. Put all the vegetables, including the onion rings and ½ cup parsley, into ice water and let stand for about 1 hour. Drain and spindry in a salad spinner, or dry with kitchen towels. Combine the vegetables with dressing shortly before serving.

4 When the salad is dressed, turn it out on a round or oval platter and mound it so that it resembles a melon. Garnish with remaining parsley and red and green pepper strips.

Dandelion Salad with Smoked Turkey

SERVES 4

Connoisseurs rave over dandelion sprouts, and when asked why they usually mention its wonderful bitter flavor — akin to arugula, though in our opinion the latter is markedly stronger. Our Mama Angela, in her 86th year, still picks fresh dandelions every spring and prepares them in a variety of ways, especially in simple salads. Her advice is to pick young leaves before they flower; if they have already flowered, the bitterness is pronounced and the leaves are tough. Actually, most greengrocers sell young, fresh dandelion these days.

> *2 pounds dandelion leaves*
> *6 tablespoons olive oil*
> *2 tablespoons white wine vinegar*
> *salt*
> *freshly ground pepper*
> *8 ounces smoked turkey breast, sliced*
> *   as thinly as possible*

1 Wash the dandelion leaves carefully and dry as well as possible; draining in a colander and then laying them in batches on cotton or linen toweling and patting them with additional toweling is one of the simplest and best ways. This can be done ahead of time; when leaves are dried, put them in plastic bags, tie the bags and refrigerate.

2 Combine oil, vinegar, salt, and pepper and blend thoroughly. Pour over dandelion leaves and toss lightly but well. Roll the turkey slices into cylinders and arrange at edge of serving plates or platter. Serve as soon as dandelion is tossed with dressing

Avocado with Lobster and Radish Angel Hair

SERVES 4

20 white radishes
10 red radishes
salt
6 tablespoons olive oil
4 tablespoons fresh lemon juice
3 green onions, thinly sliced
salt
freshly ground pepper

1½ cups cooked lobster meat cut into
   1-inch pieces, or use 11.3-ounce
   canned or frozen lobster
½ cup homemade Mayonnaise
   (page 261)
1 teaspoon capers
3 avocados

1 Scrub radishes, trim ends and place radishes in a bowl. Salt liberally, fill bowl with water and ice cubes, and refrigerate 1 hour.

2 Drain, pat dry, and shred radishes as finely as possible on thinnest shredder of food processor.

3 Combine olive oil, 2 tablespoons lemon juice, green onions, salt, and pepper and mix well. Pour over radishes and toss lightly but thoroughly. Refrigerate until ready to use.

4 Put lobster pieces in a bowl. Add remaining lemon juice and toss. Add mayonnaise and capers and toss well to coat lobster. Set aside; refrigerate if not using right away.

5 Cut avocados in half lengthwise, remove pits, and peel. Cut away a very thin slice on outside of each half; reserve. Fill centers with lobster mixture and then with radish slivers, overflowing one side of avocado. Top with reserved thin avocado slice.

Lentil and Vegetable Salad

SERVES 4

8 ounces dried lentils
1 garlic clove
4 cups water
8 ounces green beans
1 large red bell pepper
½ cup olive oil
1 teaspoon Dijon mustard

1 tablespoon chopped fresh chervil or
   1 teaspoon dried
salt
freshly ground pepper
¼ cup red wine vinegar
2 bunches green onions, trimmed (save
   the green tops for another use)

1 Wash and pick over the lentils. In a medium saucepan combine lentils and garlic clove with 4 cups water. Bring to a fast boil, lower heat, and simmer 30 minutes, stirring now and then. Drain and rinse lentils with cold water. Discard garlic. Set lentils aside.

2 Wash the green beans and lay them in a steamer. Cover and steam for 2 to 3 minutes; they should remain firm. Remove from steamer and let cool. Cut the beans into 2-inch lengths and set aside.

3 Core and seed the red pepper; cut into $2 \times \frac{1}{4}$-inch julienne. Set aside.

4 In a medium bowl combine olive oil, mustard, chervil, salt, and pepper and mix. Add the vinegar and whisk until slightly thickened. Add ½ of the vinaigrette to lentils. Adjust salt and pepper to taste. Let the lentils marinate for a few hours.

5 Place the lentils in the middle of a large platter. Arrange beans, red pepper, and green onions into little bundles (make sure they are all the same length). If you wish, blanch the green parts of the onions, cut into thin strips, and lay 2 strips criss-cross on each bundle. Set the vegetable bundles around the lentils. When ready to serve, pour the remaining vinaigrette overall.

Broccoli and Brown Rice Salad

❦

SERVES 4 TO 6

See photo 4 following page 220.

2½ cups chicken stock or vegetable broth
1 cup brown rice
3 cups water
12 ounces broccoli, stems peeled and
 sliced crosswise
1 carrot, thinly sliced with a vegetable
 peeler
1 small red bell pepper, cored, seeded,
 and cut into ½-inch squares
6 green onions (including tender green
 part), finely chopped
½ cup almonds, whole or broken

½ cup olive oil
¼ cup balsamic vinegar
¼ cup fresh lemon juice
2 tablespoons finely chopped lemon zest
1 garlic clove, finely chopped
1 tablespoon finely chopped fresh
 tarragon or 1 teaspoon dried
salt
freshly ground pepper
¼ cup chopped fresh parsley
6 large radishes with leaves (garnish)

1 In a saucepan with a tight-fitting lid bring the stock or broth to a fast boil. Add the rice and cover. Lower heat and simmer 50 minutes or until liquid is absorbed. Transfer the rice to a bowl and chill it for 1 hour.

2 Bring 3 cups water to boil in medium saucepan. Add the broccoli flowerets and sliced stems and cook uncovered for 5 minutes or until crisp-tender. Drain and run cold water over the broccoli. Drain again.

3 In a large bowl combine the broccoli, carrot, red pepper, green onions, almonds, and chilled brown rice. Set aside. In a small bowl combine olive oil, vinegar, lemon juice, lemon zest, garlic, tarragon, and salt and pepper to taste and whisk thoroughly. Pour one half of the dressing onto the broccoli mixture and blend well. Taste and adjust seasoning. Chill, covered, for 1 hour.

4 Transfer salad to a large serving platter and add the remaining dressing. Sprinkle with chopped parsley and garnish with radishes.

Tofu Garden Salad

SERVES 2 TO 4

1 cucumber, ends trimmed and most
  of skin peeled, seeds removed if
  necessary, very thinly sliced
1 carrot, cut into julienne
2 small bell or frying peppers, cored,
  seeded, and cut into julienne
1 large ripe tomato, cored, blanched
  for 2 minutes, peeled, seeded, and
  cut into ½-inch pieces
1 package (4 ounces) enoki mushrooms
4 ounces bean sprouts, blanched and
  drained well

4 ounces whole snow peas, ends
  trimmed
½ cake tofu, cut into ½-inch cubes
3 tablespoons vegetable oil

DRESSING
(makes about 1 cup)
¼ cup sugar
⅔ cup rice or white wine vinegar
1 tablespoon soy sauce
1½ teaspoons sesame oil
2 teaspoons salt
freshly ground pepper

1 For dressing, combine sugar, vinegar, soy sauce, sesame oil, salt, and
pepper to taste and blend well.

2 Sauté tofu pieces in hot vegetable oil until they turn light brown at the
edges, about 5 minutes. Drain on paper toweling.

3 Add tofu to vegetables, add dressing, toss lightly but well, and serve.

Assorted Salad Plates

The following nine salad recipes count heavily on one main ingredient. The objective is to make several and arrange two, three, or four of them on individual salad plates.

For example, a plate of Romaine Lettuce Hearts with Garlic Butter, Uncooked Tomatoes with Basil and Cream, and Sweet Red Pepper Strips with Enoki Mushrooms will make a full entree if supplemented with a soup and a substantial dessert. Of course, each of these dishes can also be served individually as accompaniments to most dishes in this book.

Romaine Lettuce Hearts with Garlic Butter

SERVES 4

4 heads romaine lettuce (Bibb or
   Boston lettuce or curly endive may
   be substituted)
4 tablespoons (½ stick) butter

2 garlic cloves, halved
1 tablespoon sugar
salt
freshly ground pepper

1 Remove all the outer leaves from lettuce, reserving them for another use. Cut away stem end of hearts and refresh under cool water if necessary; dry thoroughly. Crisp them further, if you wish, by putting them in a plastic bag and refrigerating.

2 Just before serving, melt butter in a small skillet and add garlic and sugar. Stir and cook until garlic begins to color. Remove and discard garlic. Add salt and pepper and pour hot garlic butter over cool lettuce hearts. Serve immediately.

Uncooked Tomatoes with Basil and Cream

SERVES 4

4 medium to large ripe tomatoes
½ cup whipping cream
salt
freshly ground pepper
¼ cup finely chopped fresh basil

1 Core the tomatoes and blanch them in boiling water just long enough to loosen skins, 1 to 2 minutes depending on ripeness. Drain tomatoes, run under cold water, and remove skins. Slice as thinly as you can and arrange slices on a plate.

2 Pour cream overall. Salt and pepper liberally and sprinkle with basil. Serve immediately.

Carrot Strips with Mustard and Herbs

SERVES 4

1 pound carrots, peeled and cut into
   3 × ¼-inch julienne
1 cup dry white wine
1 cup white wine vinegar
½ cup water
¼ cup olive oil
1 tablespoon sugar
1 teaspoon salt

1 bay leaf
2 tablespoons chopped fresh oregano or
   1 teaspoon dried
2 tablespoons chopped fresh parsley
1 large garlic clove, minced
¼ teaspoon red pepper flakes
1 teaspoon Dijon mustard

1 Leave julienned carrots in cool water until ready to cook.

2 In a medium saucepan combine all other ingredients except mustard. Cover and bring them to boil, then lower heat and simmer about 10 minutes. Strain and return liquid to saucepan.

3 Cook carrots in the wine mixture until crisp-tender. Drain, reserving liquid. Whisk the mustard into the liquid and pour over carrots. Toss well. Marinate carrots in refrigerator overnight or up to a week. Remove from refrigerator, bring to room temperature, and toss several times before serving.

Whole Leeks with Butter and Nutmeg

SERVES 4

8 small or 4 medium to large leeks,
*   tough green ends cut away, washed*
*   thoroughly*
2 tablespoons unsalted butter, melted
pinch of freshly grated nutmeg
salt
freshly ground pepper

1 Boil leeks in a large skillet half filled with salted water until tender but not mushy. Test for doneness by piercing a leek with knife or fork. Drain and pat dry.

2 Pour warm melted butter over leeks and sprinkle lightly with nutmeg (be careful not to overdo the nutmeg; a hint is all that is needed). Serve right away.

Young Fresh Spinach with Toasted Sesame Dressing

SERVES 4

2 pounds fresh spinach
¼ cup sesame seed
1 teaspoon sugar
4 teaspoons soy sauce
¼ cup dashi (see note), chicken stock,
  or vegetable broth

1 Remove outer thick leaves from spinach bunches and reserve for another use; use only the smaller leaves in this recipe. Wash well, drain, dry, and set aside. You should have about 1 pound spinach leaves.

2 Toast sesame seed in a small ungreased skillet over low heat, stirring and shaking pan very frequently. As soon as seeds begin to turn golden, remove from heat and transfer to a mortar or blender. Add sugar and grind seeds to powder. Transfer to a small bowl and add soy sauce and *dashi* or stock. Mix well, pour over spinach leaves and toss.

NOTE
*D*ashi is Japan's popular fish-based soup stock and seasoning. It is available at some shops in instant cube form. If you can't get it, use chicken stock or vegetable broth.

Celery Curls and Radish Sprouts with Orange Zest

SERVES 4

The vegetables can be prepared early in the day and put in a plastic bag in the refrigerator until ready to use. Dressing should be made ahead and left at room temperature for an hour or longer.

1 bunch celery (remove outer stalks),
  washed, strings removed, dried, and
  shredded on small holes of hand
  grater or food processor (about 3 cups)
½ cup (one 2.5-ounce package) radish
  sprouts, washed and dried
1 bunch watercress, stemmed, washed,
  and dried
4 green onions, thinly sliced

¼ cup finely chopped fresh parsley
½ cup olive oil
3 tablespoons raspberry vinegar
2 teaspoons chopped orange zest
1 garlic clove, finely chopped
salt
freshly ground pepper
8 slices fresh ripe tomato
12 oil-cured black or green olives, pitted

1 Combine celery, radish sprouts, watercress, green onions, and parsley in large bowl.

2 In small bowl combine olive oil, raspberry vinegar, orange zest, garlic, salt, and pepper and mix well. Pour over salad greens and toss lightly but thoroughly.

3 Arrange tomato slices on serving platter and place salad on top, showing some of the tomato. Scatter olives on top. Serve immediately.

Sweet Red Pepper Strips with Enoki Mushrooms

SERVES 4

See photo 2 following page 28.

4 large red bell peppers
¼ cup olive oil
2 tablespoons white wine vinegar
1 garlic clove, minced
½ teaspoon finely chopped fresh basil
  or a pinch of dried

1 teaspoon finely chopped fresh
  oregano or ½ teaspoon dried
salt
freshly ground pepper
1 package (4 ounces) enoki
  mushrooms

1 Wipe the peppers clean with a damp cloth. Place them on a rimmed baking sheet and broil them under a low flame until the skins are charred on all sides. Put the peppers in a brown paper bag, close the end of the bag and set aside to cool for 10 minutes. Shake the bag; this will help loosen the skins. Set aside.

2 Combine all ingredients except the red peppers and mushrooms in a small bowl and whisk until well blended. Leave at room temperature until ready to pour over red pepper strips.

3 Peel off the skins when the peppers are cool enough to handle. Remove cores and seeds. Cut the peppers into ½-inch-wide strips. Arrange on serving plate and distribute enoki mushrooms over peppers. Pour on oil and vinegar dressing and serve.

Pearl Onion Salad with Raspberry Vinegar

SERVES 4

10 ounces fresh pearl onions, peeled and cooked until tender, or one 10-ounce package frozen pearl onions, cooked until tender
1 tablespoon butter
1 teaspoon sugar
¼ cup olive oil

2 teaspoons raspberry vinegar
1 teaspoon finely chopped fresh thyme or ½ teaspoon dried
2 tablespoons dried currants
1 cup fresh tomato cut into ½-inch cubes
salt
freshly ground pepper

1 Sauté cooked onions in the butter and sugar until nicely coated; keep stirring or shaking pan until onions are lightly caramelized. Remove from heat and transfer to mixing bowl.

2 Add olive oil, raspberry vinegar, thyme, currants, tomato, salt, and pepper; let cool. Taste and adjust seasoning. These may be refrigerated up to a week, but be sure to bring to room temperature before serving.

Cucumbers in Mint and Ice

SERVES 4

This is a refreshing, delightful, and heavenly scented dish. Please use young cucumbers.

4 young, slender cucumbers
1 tablespoon salt
4 full sprigs fresh mint
2 cups cold water
2 cups ice cubes

1 Slice off ends of cucumbers and peel 90% of the skin away with a vegetable peeler. Run the tines of a fork up and down the full length of the cucumbers. Cut cucumbers in eighths lengthwise; if you're using mature cucumbers, you will have to scoop out the overgrown seeds.

2 In a bowl wide enough to contain the cucumber lengths, combine them with salt, mint, water, and ice cubes. Let stand in or out of refrigerator for 1 hour to crisp and scent cucumbers.

3 Serve in bowl, just as they are. This is one time you don't have to drain and dry a vegetable.

12

SOUPS – MOSTLY THICK AND HEARTY

Food and eating styles are changing, to everyone's advantage and better health. But along with bread, one food remains constant and popular: Soup! "*Je vis de bonne soupe, et non de beau langage,*" said Molière; "I live by good soup, and not by fine words." Well, not just Molière. Soup could not be soup without vegetables. Even the lightest, clearest consomme is enriched by the use of certain vegetables, for they are the aromatics. In the good old days formal dinners, as a rule, included two soups, one thin and one thick — and for many years this has been the way in which most cookbooks classify or categorize soups.

Thin, clear soups are also known as consommes; they may be liquid or jellied, hot or cold. Thick soups have undergone some transformation in recent years, and are now often thickened with vegetable puree rather than with white sauce, tapioca, rice, bread, or egg yolks. Often, though, the vegetable puree is enriched with another traditional thickener, cream.

Thick soups are more popular than ever today. They are healthy and easy to make; they get better with time, can be reheated easily, and may be the main course of the meal. Almost any vegetable or combination will make a good soup. Although the literature bulges with vegetable soup recipes, here are some of our favorites.

Opposite: Mosaic Vegetable Terrine (page 80).
Following page: Crepes Filled with a Spinach
and Cheese Souffle (page 131).

Fresh Fava Bean Soup

SERVES 6

3 pounds fresh fava beans, shelled
2 small boiling potatoes, cut into
    ½-inch cubes
2 cups chicken stock
1 cup water
salt
freshly ground pepper

1 cup (about) light cream
4 ounces smoked ham or bacon
1 large garlic clove, minced
½ cup finely chopped green onions
½ cup finely chopped fresh parsley
2 tablespoons butter

1 In a large saucepan combine the favas, potatoes, chicken stock, and water and bring to boil. Cover the pan, lower the heat, and simmer until beans are tender, about 40 to 45 minutes. Put vegetables and liquid through a food mill; do not use a food processor, as it will puree too finely. Add salt and pepper as needed and thin the soup with light cream to desired consistency (the soup should be fairly thick).

2 Chop the ham or bacon into ½-inch pieces and combine with the garlic, green onions, and parsley. Melt the butter in a skillet and sauté the ham or bacon mixture for several minutes, or until the ham pieces brown at the edges or the bacon is done.

3 Divide the soup among 6 bowls and top with ham or bacon mixture. Serve hot.

Opposite: Broccoli and Brown Rice Salad (page 210).
Preceding page: Gazpacho Terrine—A Cold
Vegetable Pâté (page 74).

Vegetable Bean Soup with Pistou

SERVES 10 TO 12

See photo 3 following page 172.

4 cups water
1 cup dried Great Northern or navy
  beans
6 tablespoons olive oil
1 large onion, coarsely chopped
3 cups cored, blanched, peeled, seeded,
  and chopped fresh tomatoes, or
  3 cups canned plum tomatoes,
  seeded and chopped
3½ quarts water
1 tablespoon salt
2 carrots, peeled and cut into ¼-inch
  slices
2 cups boiling potatoes cut into ½-inch
  cubes
1 cup coarsely chopped leeks
2 stalks celery with leaves, coarsely
  chopped

2 cups green beans cut into 2-inch
  lengths
2 cups zucchini cut into ⅛-inch slices
  (do not peel)
½ cup small shells or other small pasta
⅛ teaspoon powdered saffron or
  crumbled saffron threads
1 cup freshly grated Parmesan cheese

PISTOU
3 large garlic cloves, minced
½ teaspoon salt
¼ cup chopped fresh parsley
¼ cup chopped fresh basil or
  2 tablespoons dried
¼ cup olive oil
½ cup freshly grated Parmesan cheese

1 Bring 4 cups water to boil in 6-quart pot. Add the beans and boil for 3 minutes. Turn the heat off and let the beans soak for 1 hour. Return to high heat and bring the water to a full boil. Lower the heat and simmer the beans for 1 hour or until tender. Drain the beans.

2 Heat olive oil in the same pot in which the beans were cooked. Sauté the onion over medium heat for 2 minutes; do not let onion brown. Add the tomatoes and bring to a boil. Lower heat and cook for 5 minutes. Add 3½ quarts water and salt and return soup to boil. Add the carrots, potatoes, leeks, and celery. Lower the heat again and cook for 15 minutes. Add the green beans, zucchini, cooked white beans, and pasta and cook for 10 to 15 minutes longer; the vegetables should not be too soft. Add the saffron and cook 1 to 2 minutes more.

3 For *pistou*, combine garlic, salt, parsley, and basil in heavy bowl and mash with the back of a wooden spoon. Add the olive oil a little at a time, mashing with the spoon until mixture is smooth. Stir in grated Parmesan and mix well. Cover with foil and set aside until the soup is done.

4 Before serving, add the *pistou* and mix well. Adjust seasoning. Pass grated Parmesan separately.

Lentil Soup with Swiss Chard

SERVES 6

1 pound dried lentils
3 tablespoons butter
2 medium onions, coarsely chopped
2 carrots, peeled and cut into ¼-inch
   slices
2 garlic cloves, coarsely chopped
3 quarts chicken stock or vegetable broth
1 bay leaf

1 cup cooked chopped Swiss chard,
   including stems
¼ cup fresh lemon juice
salt
freshly ground pepper
1 lemon, sliced as thinly as possible,
   seeded

1 Pick over the lentils carefully to remove any pebbles or other foreign particles. Wash several times in cool water and drain. Set aside.

2 Melt the butter in a large casserole over medium-low heat. Add the onions, carrots, and garlic and cook until onions are soft, about 5 minutes. Add the lentils, stock or broth, and bay leaf. Bring mixture to boil, reduce the heat, and simmer 1 hour or until the lentils are cooked.

3 Add the Swiss chard and lemon juice and return to boil. Lower the heat and simmer for 5 minutes. Adjust the seasoning with salt and pepper and serve in individual bowls, each with a slice of lemon.

Cool Green Pea Soup with Mint and Tarragon

SERVES 6

1 cup water
1 teaspoon salt
2 cups fresh peas or one 10-ounce
  package frozen
3 cups chicken stock or vegetable broth
1 teaspoon chopped fresh mint or
  ½ teaspoon dried
1 teaspoon chopped fresh tarragon or
  1 teaspoon dried

1 cup dry white wine
2 tablespoons butter, softened
1½ tablespoons all-purpose flour
1 cup whipping cream
salt
freshly ground pepper
2 tablespoons chopped fresh chives or
  1 teaspoon dried

1 Bring 1 cup water to boil in a saucepan and add the salt. Add the peas and cook until tender, about 5 to 10 minutes. Drain the peas and transfer to a large mixing bowl. Add the stock or broth, mint, and tarragon, then puree mixture in batches in a blender, processor, or food mill. Transfer puree to a large saucepan. Add wine and cook over moderate heat for 10 minutes, stirring frequently.

2 Meanwhile, combine butter and flour in a cup and blend well. Add to the hot soup and bring slowly to boil. Reduce heat and simmer until soup thickens, about 5 to 10 minutes. If you would like to serve soup hot, add the cream after the soup has thickened and heat just to boiling point. To serve cold, remove the saucepan from the heat, transfer its contents to a glass or ceramic bowl, and refrigerate the soup until cold.

Before serving, stir in cream and adjust seasoning. Sprinkle with chopped chives.

Fresh Basil and Tomato Soup

SERVES 6

See photo 1 following page 188.

1 sweet Italian sausage
1 teaspoon olive oil
1 garlic clove, halved
1 large leek, cut into ½-inch pieces
1 large stalk celery with leaves, cut
  into ½-inch pieces
1 large onion, thinly sliced
1 tablespoon sugar

2 pounds fresh tomatoes, cored,
  blanched, peeled, and coarsely
  chopped
3 cups beef stock
salt
freshly ground pepper
juice of 1 lemon
6 tablespoons chopped fresh basil

1 In a heavy large saucepan sauté sausage link in the olive oil until well done, about 10 minutes. Remove the sausage and set aside. There should be 2 tablespoons oil and fat left in the saucepan. If there is more, pour off excess; if not enough, add a bit of butter. Add garlic and cook until light brown. Press down on the garlic with a wooden spoon to extract juice, then discard.

2 Add the leek, celery, and onion and sauté for about 10 minutes. Add sugar, tomatoes, sausage, and stock and bring the mixture to a boil. Reduce heat and simmer for 30 minutes.

3 Remove the sausage and put the soup through food mill (do not use blender or processor for this, because a food mill will remove most of the tomato seeds and provide a better texture). Add salt and pepper to taste.

4 Cut the sausage link into the thinnest possible slices. Cut each slice into quarters and add them to the soup. Add the lemon juice and 4 tablespoons basil and cook the soup for 2 more minutes. Serve in individual bowls with a sprinkle of the remaining basil.

Corn and Lettuce Soup

SERVES 6

4 ears fresh corn or 1 cup frozen or
   canned corn kernels
2 tablespoons corn oil
4 tablespoons (½ stick) butter
1 large onion, finely chopped
2 garlic cloves, finely chopped
4 fresh tomatoes, cored, blanched,
   peeled, and finely chopped, or 2 cups
   canned plum tomatoes

8 cups very finely shredded lettuce
4 cups beef stock
3 tablespoons chopped fresh chervil or
   1 tablespoon dried
salt
freshly ground pepper.
3 tablespoons grated Cheddar cheese

1 Shuck the corn, drop the cobs into boiling salted water, and cook them for 7 minutes. Remove corn, cool, cut the kernels off the cobs, and set aside.

2 Heat oil and butter in a large saucepan. Add the onion and cook slowly until onion is softened and begins to turn light brown. Add garlic and cook 2 minutes, stirring frequently.

3 Add the tomatoes, lettuce, stock, and chervil and simmer until the lettuce slices are tender (use a fork or slotted spoon to take out a piece and test for doneness; do not overcook). Add the corn, taste, and season with salt and pepper.

4 Sprinkle ½ tablespoon Cheddar cheese over each bowl of soup, or sprinkle all the cheese over the soup in a tureen. Serve with hot buttered corn sticks or corn bread.

Minestrone Soup

SERVES 6 TO 8

3 tablespoons olive oil
2 tablespoons butter
2 small boiling potatoes, peeled and
 cut into ½-inch cubes
2 garlic cloves, finely chopped
2 medium onions, finely chopped
4 large tomatoes, cored, blanched,
 peeled, and diced, or 2 cups canned
 plum tomatoes
6 cups beef or vegetable stock
3 small zucchini (unpeeled), thinly
 sliced (about 2 cups)
2 cups shelled fresh peas or one
 10-ounce package frozen
2 cups shelled fresh lima beans or one
 10-ounce package frozen
4 stalks celery with leaves, thinly sliced
2 carrots, thinly sliced
2 fresh cherry peppers or 1 dried chili
 pepper

2 tablespoons chopped fresh basil or
 1 teaspoon dried
2 tablespoons fresh parsley or
 1 teaspoon dried
salt
freshly ground pepper
freshly grated Parmesan cheese

BREAD BALLS
1 cup fresh breadcrumbs
¼ cup finely diced cooked ham
¼ cup plus 2 tablespoons freshly grated
 Parmesan cheese
1 tablespoon finely chopped fresh parsley
1 teaspoon dried oregano
1 egg, lightly beaten
¼ cup milk
salt
freshly ground pepper

1 Heat olive oil and butter in a large, deep saucepan. Add potato cubes and sauté for 5 minutes. Add the garlic and onions and cook 2 minutes longer.

2 Add the tomatoes, stock, zucchini, fresh peas, fresh lima beans, celery, carrots, cherry peppers (or chili pepper), basil, and parsley. (If you use frozen limas and peas, add them 20 minutes after you add the other vegetables.) Cover the saucepan and cook over low heat, stirring frequently, for 40 minutes, or until the lima beans are tender.

3 For bread balls, mix all ingredients in a medium bowl. Make tiny balls (no larger than 1 inch) from mixture; you should have about 20. Set the bread balls aside until you are ready to add them to soup.

4 About 10 minutes before the vegetables have finished cooking, add the bread balls. Add salt to taste along with pepper freshly ground from a mill, an important complement to the various fresh vegetables in this soup.

5 Pass the Parmesan cheese separately; a tablespoon of Parmesan added to each bowl is the finishing touch.

Vegetable Cream Soup

SERVES 6

8 tablespoons (1 stick) butter
4 small or 2 large leeks, washed
  thoroughly and thickly sliced
3 cups cooked vegetables (combine as
  many as you can, e.g., broccoli,
  Brussels sprouts, zucchini, carrots,
  green beans, peas, celery, cabbage,
  or any other vegetables you have on
  hand)
2 tablespoons all-purpose flour

3 cups chicken stock or vegetable broth
2 teaspoons sugar
1 tablespoon finely chopped fresh
  tarragon or ½ teaspoon dried
½ cup whipping cream or light cream
2 tablespoons dry Sherry
salt
freshly ground pepper
¼ cup chopped fresh parsley

1 Melt butter in a large saucepan or flameproof casserole and sauté the leeks and vegetables for about 6 minutes. Sprinkle flour overall, stir, and cook for 2 minutes more.

2 Add stock or broth, sugar, and tarragon, stirring constantly. Bring to a boil, lower heat, cover, and cook 12 minutes.

3 Puree mixture in food mill or processor. Return to pan in which it cooked, add the cream, Sherry, and salt and pepper to taste, and bring just to boiling point but do not boil. Thin with more cream or chicken stock if you wish. Sprinkle with fresh parsley and serve hot. The soup is also very good cold. Just cool and refrigerate it after cooking as above; sprinkle with parsley just before serving.

Fiddlehead and Onion Soup

SERVES 6

4 tablespoons (½ stick) unsalted butter
½ cup chopped shallots
½ cup chopped onion
2 cups boiling potatoes, peeled and cut
  into ½-inch cubes
1 quart chicken stock or vegetable broth

salt
freshly ground pepper
2 cups fiddleheads, cleaned (see note)
1 cup (about) light cream
¼ cup chopped fresh chives

1 Melt butter in a large saucepan, add the shallots and onions, and sauté for 2 minutes. Dry the potato cubes and add to the saucepan. Toss them with the shallots and onions and sauté 3 to 4 minutes. Add the stock with salt and pepper to taste. Bring the mixture to a rapid boil, lower heat, and simmer gently for 35 minutes, or until the vegetables are tender.

2 Puree the mixture in batches in a blender or food processor, or put it through a food mill. Return to the saucepan and add the fiddleheads. Simmer for 3 minutes, then add cream to achieve the desired thickness. Taste and adjust seasoning. Sprinkle chopped chives on each serving.

NOTE

Fiddleheads can be bought in specialty markets in the spring. Wash fresh fiddleheads and soak in cold water, changing the water 3 or 4 times, to remove any grit. Drain. Fiddleheads can be wrapped and refrigerated up to one week or they can be blanched and frozen.

Classic Gazpacho

SERVES 6

This is an all-vegetable dish, loaded with freshness and goodness.

6 medium-size very ripe tomatoes, cored, blanched, peeled, seeded, and coarsely chopped
1 large onion, coarsely chopped
2 medium cucumbers, peeled and coarsely chopped
1 large green bell pepper, cored, seeded, and coarsely chopped
3 garlic cloves, coarsely chopped
3 cups coarse fresh Italian or French breadcrumbs, crust removed
2 cups water
1/4 cup red wine vinegar
1/4 cup olive oil
1 tablespoon salt

1 teaspoon ground cumin
freshly ground pepper
2 cups tomato juice

GARNISH
6 slices Italian or French bread, rubbed with garlic and cut into 1/2-inch cubes
4 small or 2 medium cucumbers, peeled, seeded, and finely chopped
1 large Spanish or purple onion, finely chopped
1 large red bell pepper, finely chopped
1/4 cup finely chopped fresh basil

1 In a large bowl combine the tomatoes, onion, cucumbers, green pepper, garlic, bread, and 2 cups water. Mix well and let stand 10 minutes.

2 Puree the mixture in batches in blender or food processor (do not puree too finely; the mixture should have texture). Transfer to a large bowl.

3 In the same blender or processor combine the vinegar, olive oil, salt, cumin, and pepper and blend for a few seconds.

4 Add the vinegar mixture to the tomato puree. Add tomato juice and blend well. Taste for seasoning.

5 Cover the soup and refrigerate for 4 to 5 hours, or until ice cold.

6 About 15 to 20 minutes before serving preheat the oven to 300°F. Toast the bread cubes for garnish in the oven until crisp.

7 Stir up the gazpacho and serve in individual clear glass bowls or mugs. Put the bread cubes and finely chopped vegetables in separate bowls and pass along with the soup. Each guest may spoon into the soup what is desired.

White Almond Gazpacho

SERVES 6

This is different and very good. Not as pungent as the red gazpacho, it contains neither cream nor butter.

8 ounces blanched almonds
2 large garlic cloves
2 teaspoons salt
2 4-inch-long sections of French,
    Italian, or homemade white bread
5 cups ice water
⅔ cup olive oil
¼ cup tarragon vinegar

2 cups seedless white grapes, halved
    lengthwise
1 cup diced cucumber
¼ cup thinly sliced green onions
½ cup thinly sliced white radishes
2 tablespoons lightly toasted sliced
    almonds

1 Grind the 8 ounces almonds with garlic and salt in blender or food processor. Do not remove.

2 Soak bread in cool water in a large bowl. Squeeze dry. Add to almond mixture in blender or processor with 1 cup ice water and blend well.

3 Add remaining 4 cups ice water, olive oil, and vinegar and puree. (If using a blender, you will have to do this in several batches; in processor, two batches will suffice.)

4 Transfer to large glass or ceramic bowl and add grapes, cucumber, green onion, and radishes. Refrigerate for several hours or, better still, overnight. Just before serving add toasted almond slices.

Chinese Cabbage Soup with Cucumbers

SERVES 4

4 dried Chinese mushrooms
1 tablespoon vegetable oil
1 tablespoon sesame oil
1 whole chicken breast, boned,
   skinned, and thinly sliced
½ cup thinly sliced green onions
½ cup finely chopped celery with leaves
¼ cup thinly sliced bamboo shoots
2 cups finely shredded Chinese cabbage

1 garlic clove, finely chopped
1 teaspoon grated fresh ginger
1 tablespoon soy sauce
2 tablespoons dry Sherry
6 cups chicken stock
1 cup water
1 teaspoon Chinese sesame oil
1 small cucumber, peeled and very
   thinly sliced (garnish)

1 Wash mushrooms and soak in warm water to cover for 1 hour. Drain and slice; set aside.

2 Heat 1 tablespoon each of vegetable and sesame oil in large saucepan and sauté the chicken for 2 minutes. Remove chicken and set aside.

3 In the same saucepan, sauté the green onions, celery, bamboo shoots, cabbage, and garlic for 2 minutes. Add the ginger, soy sauce, Sherry, chicken broth, and water.

4 Transfer the chicken to the soup pot. Bring soup to a fast boil, lower heat and simmer 5 minutes. Add the soaked mushrooms and simmer an additional 2 minutes. Stir in 1 teaspoon sesame oil.

5 Serve in individual bowls, garnishing each serving with 3 or 4 cucumber slices.

13

VEGETABLE SANDWICHES, PIZZAS AND CALZONI

Most of us know that bread has been a synonym for life throughout the history of mankind. In our family bread was considered sacred. To this day, our 86-year-old mother admonishes any of us who sits to eat with bread absent from the table. Yes, we grew up with an abundance of vegetables, but bread was always there, too. *That* is what inspired this chapter.

Freshly cooked broccoli, spinach, Swiss chard, burdock, or other greens were often served on top of homemade bread in the form of an open sandwich. Homemade day-old bread was topped with fresh tomatoes, basil, onions, and many other fresh vegetables. Pizzas were crowned with peppers, mushrooms, onions — whatever fresh vegetable was on hand.

Calzoni, which are really pizza dough folded over and filled, are traditionally stuffed with cured meats, cheeses, and eggs, but in our home there were always variations — in other words, calzoni were filled with surprises, some of which are included here. Calzoni literally means "breeches," trousers which come just below the knee (or as we used to think, just cover the buttocks. This always caused a teenage giggle). In any case, they make a wonderful "sandwich" in a way similar to pita bread.

Where produce is concerned, the pride and joy of any cook should be the first of the crop. If that is simply not attainable, then let's seek young, small fresh vegetables. As Americans, we still like things in big packages — big cars, big refrigerators, big houses. But try, if you will, to choose small vegetables at the greengrocer's if you can't pick them this way from your own vines and bushes. Sandwich fillings, pizza toppings and calzone stuffings will always be better if the vegetables are young and fresh.

Broccoli Rabe with Goat Cheese

SERVES 6

2½ pounds broccoli rabe
2 to 3 cups water
salt
¾ cup broccoli cooking liquid
⅓ cup olive oil
1 garlic clove, finely chopped

1 dried chili pepper (optional)
freshly ground pepper
6 thick slices French or Italian bread,
  toasted
6 tablespoons goat cheese

1 Wash the broccoli rabe well and trim the stem ends. Peel the strings on the larger stalks just as you would on a large celery stalk. Cut the larger leaves in half. If you are not ready to cook them, let stand in cool water.

2 In a large saucepan bring 2 to 3 cups water to boil with 1 teaspoon salt. Add the broccoli rabe and cook until just tender; depending on the size and freshness of the stalks, this will take 5 to 10 minutes. Drain, reserving ¾ cup liquid. Transfer broccoli to a bowl.

3 Heat the olive oil in a large saucepan and sauté the garlic until it turns pale yellow; do not let it brown. Discard garlic. Add the chili pepper to the oil if you wish, then add the cooked broccoli and reserved cooking liquid (be careful; hot oil will sizzle and splatter). Bring to boil, then remove from heat; do not overcook. Add salt and pepper.

4 Place a slice of bread on each serving plate or arrange them all on a large platter. Put broccoli on top of the bread and spoon any remaining juice overall. Add 1 tablespoon cheese to each slice and run under broiler to melt cheese. Serve immediately.

Oven Spinach Sandwich

SERVES 4

1½ cups cooked fresh spinach or one
   10-ounce package frozen
4 tablespoons (½ stick) butter
3 tablespoons finely chopped onion
2 tablespoons finely chopped shallot
1 tablespoon chopped fresh dill or
   1 teaspoon dried
salt
freshly ground pepper

6 thin slices Italian or French bread
   (if the bread slices are small, cut
   enough to fit the baking dish), crust
   removed
3 eggs
1½ cups light cream
1 teaspoon dried chervil or
   1 tablespoon fresh
4 ounces Monterey Jack or Cheddar
   cheese, shredded
4 slices bacon, cooked until crisp,
   drained, and crumbled

1 Drain spinach; squeeze out as much liquid as possible. Set aside.

2 Melt 2 tablespoons butter in a skillet, add onion and shallot, and sauté briefly. Add the spinach, dill, salt, and pepper and mix just until blended. Set aside.

3 Butter one side of each slice of bread with the remaining 2 tablespoons butter. Arrange bread buttered side up in a 12 × 8-inch baking dish. Arrange spinach on top of buttered bread.

4 In a medium bowl beat eggs, cream, chervil, and salt and pepper until blended. Pour over spinach and bread and top with cheese.

5 Bake in preheated 375°F oven for 25 minutes. Remove from oven and sprinkle the bacon evenly on top. Cut into wedges and serve.

Zucchini Pizza with Red Pepper and Cheese Topping

SERVES 6

1½ pounds small zucchini (about
   1 × 6 inches)
2 onions, grated (1 cup)
3 eggs
½ cup freshly grated Parmesan cheese
½ cup skim- or whole-milk ricotta
½ cup bread flour
1 tablespoon finely chopped fresh
   oregano or 1 teaspoon dried
juice of ½ lemon
salt

freshly ground pepper
2 tablespoons vegetable or corn oil for
   pan

TOPPING
5 ounces fontina cheese, shredded
1 red bell pepper, cored, seeded, and
   finely chopped (about 1 cup)
½ teaspoon red pepper flakes
⅓ cup finely chopped fresh parsley

1 Wash zucchini and trim ends (do not peel). Shred on large holes of hand grater or in food processor. Squeeze to remove as much water as you can; you should have approximately 4 cups of shredded zucchini. Transfer to large mixing bowl and mix in grated onions.

2 In a separate bowl beat eggs. Add Parmesan, ricotta, flour, oregano, lemon juice, and salt and pepper; mix well. Add to zucchini and onion mixture from Step 1; mix well. Transfer to 14- to 15-inch pizza pan which has been coated with 2 tablespoons oil. Spread with rubber spatula and tap pan on counter to distribute "batter" evenly. Bake in preheated 350°F oven about 30 minutes.

3 Meanwhile, for filling, combine fontina, red bell pepper, red pepper flakes, and parsley and toss lightly to blend. Sprinkle mixture on top of cooked zucchini pizza. Return to oven for 20 more minutes.

4 Let pizza cool for 10 minutes before slicing.

Pizza with Vegetable Topping

❧

SERVES 6

See photo 3 following page 124.

PIZZA DOUGH
2¹/₂ to 3 cups all-purpose flour
1 egg, room temperature
1 teaspoon salt
1 envelope dry yeast or 1 cake fresh
    yeast, dissolved in ¹/₄ cup lukewarm
    water
¹/₂ to ³/₄ cup warm water

TOMATO SAUCE
(makes about 1¹/₂ cups)
1 tablespoon olive oil
1 garlic clove, finely chopped
1¹/₂ cups cored, blanched, peeled,
    and chopped fresh tomatoes, or well-
    drained canned plum tomatoes
1 tablespoon finely chopped fresh
    basil or 1 teaspoon dried

1 teaspoon salt
1 teaspoon dried oregano

TOPPING
1 large onion, finely chopped
4 ounces small mushrooms, thinly
    sliced
4 cooked artichoke hearts, thinly sliced
1 red bell pepper, cored, seeded, and
    cut into ¹/₄-inch cubes
12 oil-cured black olives, pitted and
    coarsely chopped
2 tablespoons grated pecorino Romano
    cheese
freshly ground pepper
2 tablespoons olive oil
2 cups shredded mozzarella cheese
¹/₄ cup finely chopped fresh parsley

1 For dough, put 2½ cups flour in a large bowl and make a well in the center. In a small bowl, mix the egg, salt, and dissolved yeast. Pour this into center of flour and mix well with a wooden spoon, adding the warm water a little at a time until dough leaves the sides of the bowl. Turn dough out onto lightly floured surface and knead for 10 minutes or until smooth and elastic.

2 Transfer dough to buttered large bowl, turning to coat all sides. Let rise, covered and away from drafts, until doubled in bulk, about 1 to 1½ hours. Punch dough down and let it rise again until doubled, about 1 hour.

3 For tomato sauce, heat olive oil in a skillet and sauté the garlic for 1 minute. Add the tomatoes, basil, salt, and oregano and cook for 10 minutes. Set aside.

4 Generously butter a 12- to 14-inch pizza pan. Work the dough into the pan by flattening and shaping it to fit, making sure you push it to the outer edge and create a rim. Let the dough rest for 15 minutes.

5 Spread the tomato sauce over the dough in the pizza pan. Sprinkle the onion, mushrooms, artichoke slices, ¾ of the red bell pepper pieces, olives, and pecorino cheese overall. Season liberally with pepper; drizzle with olive oil.

6 Bake in preheated 375°F oven for 45 to 50 minutes or until the edge of the pizza is lightly browned. Remove from the oven just long enough to sprinkle mozzarella cheese overall. Add remaining red bell pepper and parsley, return pizza to oven, and bake 5 minutes longer or until mozzarella has melted. Serve hot.

Gougère with Tomato and Cumin

SERVES 6

See photo 1 following page 108.

1 cup water
8 tablespoons (1 stick) unsalted butter
½ teaspoon salt
1 cup all-purpose flour
1 cup grated Gruyère cheese
4 eggs, at room temperature
4 slices bacon, cooked until crisp, drained, and crumbled

SAUCE
(makes about ¾ cup)
3 tablespoons olive oil
2 shallots, finely chopped
1 teaspoon ground cumin
1 pound fresh ripe plum tomatoes (about 5 to 6), blanched, peeled, seeded, and cut into ½-inch cubes (see note)
salt
freshly ground pepper

1 In a medium saucepan combine water, butter, and salt and bring to boil. Add the flour and cheese and remove from heat, stirring briskly to make a dough. Add the eggs one at a time, stirring constantly. Add the bacon and mix well.

2 Butter six 4½ × 2½-inch round baking cups and half-fill the cups with the dough. With a spoon, make a well in the center; push the dough up to and around the edges of the cups.

3 Place the cups on a baking sheet and bake in preheated 375°F oven for 35 to 40 minutes, or until brown and puffy.

4 While the gougères are baking, prepare the tomato-cumin sauce. Heat the olive oil in a medium saucepan. Add the shallots and sauté for 2 minutes. Add the cumin and sauté 30 seconds. Stir in tomatoes and salt and cook for 3 to 4 minutes. Taste and adjust seasoning with salt and pepper.

5 Remove the gougères from the oven and, working quickly, spoon about 1 tablespoon sauce in the middle of each. Serve immediately.

Vegetable and Sausage Turnovers (Calzoni)

SERVES 6 TO 8

2 sweet Italian sausages
2 tablespoons oil
1 large carrot, coarsely chopped
1 cup coarsely chopped leeks
1 cup ricotta

¼ cup finely chopped fresh parsley
¼ cup freshly grated Parmesan cheese
salt
freshly ground pepper
1 recipe Calzone Dough (page 246)

1 Remove casing from the sausage. In a large saucepan heat 1 tablespoon oil over medium-high heat and brown the meat. Transfer sausage to a medium bowl.

2 Pour off all but 1 tablespoon fat from saucepan and add 1 tablespoon oil. Cook the carrot over moderate heat for 3 minutes, stirring constantly. Add the leeks and cook an additional 2 minutes. Add the vegetable mixture to the sausage along with the ricotta, parsley, Parmesan, and salt and pepper to taste. Mix well.

3 Follow directions on pages 246 – 247 on how to prepare dough and fill and bake each calzone.

Leeks, Peppers, Mushrooms, and Herbs in Calzoni

SERVES 6 TO 8

See photo 2 following page 12.

2 slices bacon
1 tablespoon olive oil
3 medium leeks, washed, dried, and
    coarsely chopped
1 medium-size red bell pepper, cored,
    seeded, and coarsely chopped
1 medium-size green bell pepper, cored,
    seeded, and coarsely chopped
8 ounces mushrooms, thinly sliced
1 large tomato, cored, blanched,
    peeled, seeded, and cut into 1/2-inch
    cubes
1 garlic clove, minced
1/2 teaspoon fennel seed
8 large pitted black olives, sliced
2 tablespoons finely chopped fresh
    basil or 1 teaspoon dried

salt
freshly ground pepper
2 cups shredded fontina cheese

CALZONE DOUGH
1 envelope dry yeast or 1 cake fresh yeast
1/4 cup warm water
31/4 cups all-purpose flour
1 teaspoon salt
1 teaspoon sugar
1 egg
1 tablespoon vegetable oil
2/3 to 3/4 cup warm water
olive oil
egg wash made of 1 egg beaten with
    1 tablespoon water

1 To make dough, dissolve yeast in 1/4 cup of warm water and set aside for 10 minutes.

2 Place 3 cups flour in a large bowl. Make a well in the center and add the salt, sugar, egg, and yeast mixture. Add the oil and warm water a little at a time, stirring with a wooden spoon until dough leaves the side of the bowl. Turn the dough out onto a lightly floured surface and knead, adding flour as necessary, 15 minutes or until smooth and elastic. Transfer to buttered large bowl and turn to coat all sides. Let dough rise, covered and away from drafts, until doubled in bulk, about 1 to 1½ hours.

3 To make filling, cook bacon slices in a large saucepan until crisp. Remove and drain on paper towels, then crumble.

4 Add 1 tablespoon olive oil to the bacon grease. Add the leeks and red and green peppers and sauté over medium-high heat for 2 minutes. Add the mushrooms and sauté for 2 minutes. Add the tomato, garlic, fennel seed, olives, and crumbled bacon and sauté for 1 minute. Let the mixture cool for 5 minutes, then add the shredded cheese. Season with salt and pepper and mix well. Set aside.

5 When the dough has risen, punch it down and let it rise again until doubled in bulk, about 1 hour. Turn it out onto a lightly floured surface and cut it in half for 2 large turnovers. Cover and let rest 15 minutes.

6 Preheat oven to 475°F. Shape each portion of dough into a ball; press down to flatten slightly. Roll out one portion of dough into 11-inch circle. Brush with olive oil. Spread half of the vegetarian mixture over half of the circle, leaving ¾-inch margin at edge. Lift up the plain half and fold it over the filling; press edges together to seal and flute with fork. Lift the calzone up carefully with a wide spatula and place on a cornmeal-sprinkled baking sheet. Repeat with other half of dough. Prick tops with a fork and brush entire top and edges of each calzone with egg wash. Bake for 20 to 25 minutes, or until nicely browned. Let the calzone sit for 10 minutes before serving.

Green Onion and Swiss Chard Calzoni

SERVES 6 TO 8

1 pound fresh Swiss chard, leaves
  separated and rinsed in cold water
3 tablespoons olive oil
8 green onions (including tender green
  parts), coarsely chopped
3 garlic cloves, minced
salt

freshly ground pepper
⅓ cup freshly grated Parmesan cheese
¼ teaspoon red pepper flakes
egg wash made of 1 egg and
  1 tablespoon water
1 tablespoon sugar
6 to 8 pats butter (1 stick), optional

1 Peel the Swiss chard stems with a vegetable peeler and cut into 2-inch lengths. In a large saucepan cook the leaves and stems in boiling salted water for 10 minutes; drain. When cool enough to handle, squeeze all the moisture from the chard. Set aside.

2 In a large saucepan heat olive oil over medium-high heat. Add the green onions and sauté for 2 minutes; add garlic and sauté 1 minute. Remove from heat and add Swiss chard, salt, pepper, Parmesan, and red pepper; toss well. Taste and adjust seasoning; set aside.

3 Follow directions on pages 246–247 on how to prepare dough and fill and bake each calzone. Brush the tops and edges with egg wash. Sprinkle the sugar overall.

4 Let the turnovers sit for 10 minutes before serving. Place a pat of butter on each plate, slice calzoni on the bias, and butter each slice if you wish.

14

BASIC RECIPES

Stocks and sauces enhance vegetable cookery. In this book we use various stocks in many ways, and give the recipes for about 50 different sauces. Stock is the nutritious foundation of many good soups and sauces. All fat should be removed before the stock is used, and this is easy to do by refrigerating it in a nonmetal bowl. The fat will rise to the top and form a thick layer which can be easily removed. In many cases veal, beef, and chicken stocks can be interchanged. We've added a fish stock as well, which you can substitute for chicken stock in certain dishes. You might try fish stock in the Fennel and Potato Stew on page 148.

STOCKS

Rich Beef Stock

MAKES ABOUT 2 QUARTS

2 pounds beef shank (meat and bones)
1 pound chicken parts (particularly necks, backbones, and, if possible, feet)
1 pound beef bones
1 pound veal bones
4 quarts water
2 leeks (including green parts), washed carefully and coarsely chopped
2 medium onions, washed but not peeled, coarsely chopped

2 stalks celery with leaves, washed and coarsely chopped
2 large carrots, scrubbed clean but not peeled, coarsely chopped
2 sprigs fresh thyme or ½ teaspoon dried
6 parsley sprigs
1 bay leaf
12 peppercorns
1 tablespoon salt

1 Combine beef shank, chicken parts, and bones in large stockpot. Cover them with water, bring to a rapid boil, and boil for 3 minutes. Remove from heat and pour off water.

2 Add all remaining ingredients to the stockpot containing the meat and bones. Bring to a boil and simmer, uncovered, for at least 3 hours. Taste for salt and pepper, but do not add any more at this time if you intend to freeze the stock for future use (after stock has been frozen the seasoning always needs to be adjusted, so wait until then to add more salt and pepper).

3 Strain the stock, using a large wooden spoon to squeeze as much juice as possible out of meat and vegetables. If the strainer is large enough, and it should be, place a small, flat plate over the meat and bones, and push down on them to extract juices.

4 If you are going to use some of the stock within the next 3 days you can keep it in the refrigerator. Freeze the rest, or all of it, in ½-cup, 1-cup, and 2-cup amounts, to use as needed. Pour measured amounts into plastic containers and freeze them overnight, then transfer the blocks of frozen stock to large plastic bags, labeling these accordingly. When you need ½ cup or 2 cups of beef stock you will have just the quantity you need. Stock will keep in the freezer indefinitely.

Rich Chicken Stock

MAKES ABOUT 2 QUARTS

1 pound veal bones, preferably with
marrow
3 pounds chicken parts — wings,
necks, gizzards, feet, hearts, backs,
and other bones
3 quarts water
2 leeks (including green parts), washed
carefully and coarsely chopped
2 medium onions, washed but not
peeled, coarsely chopped

2 large stalks celery with leaves,
washed and coarsely chopped
2 large carrots, scrubbed clean but not
peeled, coarsely chopped
8 ounces mushrooms
2 sprigs fresh thyme or 1 teaspoon dried
6 parsley sprigs
12 peppercorns
1 teaspoon salt

1 Combine the veal bones, chicken parts, and water in a large stockpot and bring to boil. Skim off the foam.

2 Add all remaining ingredients and return to boil. Lower the heat, partially cover the stockpot, and simmer the stock for at least 2 hours. Strain, refrigerate, and defat. This freezes well for 6 to 8 months.

Rich Fish Stock

MAKES ABOUT 2 QUARTS

3 tablespoons butter
3 tablespoons vegetable oil
2 leeks (including green parts), washed
carefully and coarsely chopped
2 medium onions, washed but not
peeled, coarsely chopped
2 stalks celery with leaves, washed
and coarsely chopped
2 large carrots, scrubbed clean but not
peeled, coarsely chopped

4 cups dry white wine
3 quarts water
4 pounds fish heads and bones
2 bay leaves
¼ teaspoon fennel seed
6 parsley sprigs
12 peppercorns
1 teaspoon salt

1 Heat butter and oil in a large stockpot. Add the leeks, onions, celery, and carrots and cook for about 10 minutes, or until the onions are pale yellow.

2 Add the wine, water, and fish heads and bones, and bring the liquid to a boil, skimming foam as it accumulates on the surface. Add the bay leaves, fennel, parsley, peppercorns, and salt. Stir all the ingredients well and simmer the stock, partially covered, for about 2 hours, or until liquid is reduced by half.

3 Strain, refrigerate, and defat. This may be frozen for several months.

Rich Veal Stock

MAKES ABOUT 2 QUARTS

2 pounds veal bones (not too large)
2½ pounds veal shank, cut into cubes as if for stew (or use any inexpensive veal pieces that are not too fatty)
1 calf's knuckle
2 medium onions, washed but not peeled, coarsely chopped
2 large carrots, scrubbed clean but not peeled, coarsely chopped
4 quarts water

2 large stalks celery with leaves, washed and coarsely chopped
2 leeks (including green parts), washed carefully and coarsely chopped
2 garlic cloves, coarsely chopped
2 sprigs fresh thyme or ½ teaspoon dried
6 parsley sprigs
2 bay leaves
12 peppercorns
1 tablespoon salt

1 Place the meat and bones in a large metal baking pan and brown them in a preheated 475°F to 500°F oven for 20 to 30 minutes. Reduce the heat to 400°F, add the onions and carrots, and bake for an additional 30 minutes.

2 Transfer meat, bones, and vegetables to a large stockpot and pour off fat from the baking pan. On top of the stove, deglaze the baking pan using 2 to 3 cups water from the 4 quarts. Pour this liquid into the stockpot.

3 Add all remaining ingredients and bring to boil. Lower the heat and simmer the stock uncovered for 4 hours or longer, until liquid is reduced by half.

4 Strain, refrigerate, and defat. This freezes well for months.

Opposite: Carrot Cannelloni with Vegetables (page 134).
Following page: Stuffed Tomatoes with Chicken, Peas, and Potatoes (page 126).

Meatless Vegetarian Stock

MAKES ABOUT 2 QUARTS

This stock may be used in place of meat or fish stocks. It is easy to make, will keep in refrigerator for almost a week, and may be frozen for several months.

2 large carrots, thinly sliced
2 celery stalks, thinly sliced
2 medium onions, thinly sliced
1 large or 2 small boiling potatoes,
   thinly sliced
4 parsley sprigs

1 sprig fresh thyme or ½ teaspoon dried
8 peppercorns
1 bay leaf
1 large garlic clove
½ teaspoon salt
3½ quarts of water

1 Combine all ingredients in a large saucepan with cover. If you prefer, combine peppercorns, bay leaf, garlic, and thyme in a cheesecloth square, tie ends, and add to pan for easy removal later.

2 Bring to a boil, uncovered. Lower heat, cover pan, and simmer for 1½ hours. Strain and use, store, or freeze.

Opposite: Vegetable Casserole (page 176).
Preceding page: Asparagus and Phyllo Tart
(page 99).

SAUCES

Hollandaise Sauce

MAKES ABOUT 1½ CUPS

2 tablespoons white wine vinegar
¼ cup water
1 teaspoon salt
1 teaspoon white pepper
5 or 6 eggs (depending on size), separated
1 cup (2 sticks) butter, melted
juice of ½ lemon (about 1 tablespoon)

1 In the top of a double boiler combine the vinegar, water, salt, and pepper. Over high heat, reduce the vinegar and water mixture by half, keeping the pan uncovered.

2 Remove the double boiler top from the heat, add the yolks, and whisk immediately. Place over boiling water; it should not touch the top pan. When yolks are well mixed and somewhat thickened, remove top pan from heat. Gradually whisk in butter and keep whisking until sauce is as thick as you wish it to be. Taste for seasoning and add more salt if needed. Add the lemon juice a few drops at a time, checking sauce for lemon taste along the way.

3 To keep hollandaise warm, put the double boiler top containing the sauce in a pan of warm water, or discard the hot water in the bottom pan and replace it with lukewarm water. If the hollandaise is too thick, whisk in a teaspoonful of hot water, or more if necessary, to obtain consistency you want. If the sauce is too thin, put a teaspoonful of water in a dry, warm bowl. Add a tablespoon of the thin sauce and beat hard with a wire whisk. Add another spoonful of sauce and beat. Repeat this until all the thin sauce has been incorporated.

NOTE
If the sauce separates, add a teaspoon to a tablespoon of hot water and whisk until sauce is smooth.

Sauce Bâtarde

MAKES ABOUT 2 CUPS

10½ tablespoons butter, softened
2½ tablespoons all-purpose flour
1 cup water, almost boiling
1 cup milk, scalded
2 egg yolks

¼ cup whipping cream
2 tablespoons fresh lemon juice
salt
freshly ground pepper

1 In a saucepan, melt 2½ tablespoons butter over moderate heat. Add the flour and blend well.

2 In another saucepan, mix water and milk and keep at the boiling point. Pour it slowly into the flour mixture, stirring constantly, until well blended, then cook over low heat until the sauce thickens, about 5 minutes.

3 Blend egg yolks and cream; whisk in about ¼ cup thickened sauce. Blend this mixture into sauce remaining in the saucepan and heat but do not boil.

4 Add the lemon juice and salt and pepper to taste. Whisk in remaining 8 tablespoons butter and serve.

Bechamel Sauce

MAKES ABOUT 2 CUPS

2 tablespoons butter
¼ cup all-purpose flour
2 cups milk, heated
1 parsley sprig
1 bay leaf

1 celery stalk with leaves
1 small piece carrot
¼ onion
½ teaspoon salt
white pepper

1 Melt butter in a medium saucepan. Whisk in flour and keep whisking until blended and smooth. Cook over low heat for about 2 minutes.

2 Slowly add heated milk and continue whisking until blended. Add the herbs and vegetables and cook over low heat 15 minutes. Put sauce through a fine strainer, season with salt and pepper, and serve.

Velouté Sauce

MAKES ABOUT 2 CUPS

6 tablespoons (¾ stick) butter
6 tablespoons all-purpose flour
2 cups chicken stock, heated
salt
white pepper

1 Melt the butter in a saucepan. Add flour and cook over medium heat, whisking constantly, for 2 minutes.

2 Slowly add the stock and keep whisking. Cook sauce at a simmer for about 20 minutes. Add salt and pepper to taste.

Mornay Sauce

MAKES ABOUT 2½ CUPS

2 tablespoons butter
¼ cup all-purpose flour
2 cups milk or light cream, heated
bouquet garni: 1 bay leaf, 1 celery
stalk with leaves, 1 parsley sprig,
1 small piece carrot and ½ onion
tied together in cheesecloth

½ teaspoon salt
freshly ground pepper
4 egg yolks, lightly beaten
½ cup grated Swiss cheese

1 Melt butter in a medium saucepan, add flour, and whisk until blended and smooth. Cook over low heat for 2 minutes.

2 Slowly add heated milk or cream and continue whisking. Add the bouquet garni and cook over low heat for about 8 minutes. Discard bouquet garni and add salt and pepper to taste.

3 Whisk about ½ cup sauce into egg yolks. Return mixture to saucepan, add cheese, and cook over low heat, whisking constantly, just until cheese is melted and sauce is hot and relatively smooth, about 1 to 2 minutes. Remove from heat and use the sauce as directed in recipe.

Light Tomato Sauce

MAKES ABOUT 1½ CUPS

2 pounds ripe plum tomatoes or 2 cups canned Italian plum tomatoes
8 tablespoons (1 stick) butter, cut into 8 pieces
1 medium onion, peeled and quartered
1 medium carrot, peeled and quartered
¼ teaspoon sugar
1½ teaspoons salt

1 If using fresh tomatoes, wash them well, cut each in half, and cook over low heat in a covered pan for 15 minutes. Put tomatoes through a food mill to get a fine puree. If using canned tomatoes, measure 2 cups into food mill with about ½ cup juice; again, mill to a fine puree.

2 Combine butter, onion and carrot pieces, sugar, salt, and tomato puree in a medium saucepan. Simmer over low heat for 40 minutes, uncovered; stir frequently and be sure the simmer does not turn to a boil.

3 Remove onion and carrot pieces and adjust seasoning.

NOTE
This sauce may be made ahead and reheated. It freezes very well.

Tomato Vegetable Sauce

MAKES ABOUT 3 CUPS

2 pounds ripe plum tomatoes or 2 cups
 canned plum tomatoes
⅔ cup coarsely chopped onion
⅔ cup coarsely chopped carrots
⅔ cup coarsely chopped celery,
 including some light green leaves

2 tablespoons finely chopped flat-leaf
 parsley
1 teaspoon sugar
1½ teaspoons salt
freshly ground pepper

1 Combine all ingredients in a medium saucepan.

2 Cook uncovered over low heat for 30 minutes, stirring frequently.

Old-Fashioned Spicy Tomato Sauce

MAKES ABOUT 4 CUPS

3 tablespoons olive oil
½ cup carrots cut into ¼-inch dice
½ cup onion cut into ¼- to ½-inch dice
3 pieces (1 × 2 inches) orange peel,
 finely chopped
1 tablespoon all-purpose flour
1 can (2 pounds 3 ounces) plum
 tomatoes, put through food mill with
 liquid (3½ cups)

2 garlic cloves, finely chopped
5 tablespoons sugar
3 tablespoons white wine vinegar
1 tablespoon finely chopped parsley
1 tablespoon finely chopped basil or
 1 teaspoon dried
¼ teaspoon fennel seed
¼ teaspoon red pepper flakes
1 teaspoon salt

1 Heat olive oil in saucepan, add carrots, and sauté 1 minute. Add onion and orange peel and sauté just until onion turns color. Add flour and cook 2 minutes, stirring; do not let flour scorch.

2 Add tomatoes and all remaining ingredients. Bring to boil, turn down heat and simmer uncovered for 15 minutes, stirring frequently to prevent scorching. Turn off heat and cool for 1 hour, then refrigerate.

Quick Tomato Sauce

MAKES ABOUT 2 CUPS

2 cups peeled fresh or canned
tomatoes, coarsely chopped
2 tablespoons olive oil
1 small onion, finely chopped
1 garlic clove, finely chopped

2 tablespoons finely chopped celery
leaves
1 tablespoon finely chopped fresh basil
or 1 teaspoon dried
salt
freshly ground pepper

1 Put the tomatoes through a food mill (do not puree in blender; a food mill will puree the pulp and strain out the seeds).

2 Heat the olive oil in a medium skillet or saucepan, add the onion, and sauté quickly until lightly brown. Add garlic and sauté for a few seconds. Add tomatoes, celery leaves, basil, salt, and pepper. Bring to a fast boil, lower heat to medium-high and cook for 10 minutes.

Uncooked Fresh Tomato Sauce

MAKES ABOUT 2 CUPS

3 large ripe tomatoes, cored, blanched,
peeled, seeded, and cut into ½-inch
pieces
1 garlic clove, finely chopped
1 small onion, finely chopped
8 large basil leaves, finely chopped or
1 teaspoon dried
1 tablespoon finely chopped fresh
oregano or ½ teaspoon dried

1 teaspoon finely chopped fresh
rosemary or ½ teaspoon dried,
crumbled
1½ teaspoons salt
freshly ground pepper
½ cup olive oil
Juice of 1 lemon, strained

1 Combine all ingredients and mix well.

2 This sauce can be prepared ahead of time and may be held at room temperature for as long as half a day. If made the day before, refrigerate the sauce but bring it to room temperature before serving.

Sugared Plum Tomatoes

MAKES ABOUT 2 CUPS

2 cups cored, blanched, peeled, seeded, and diced fresh tomatoes or drained canned plum tomatoes
3 tablespoons firmly packed brown sugar

1 garlic clove, minced (optional)
salt
freshly ground pepper

1 Combine all ingredients in saucepan and bring to boil.

2 Lower heat, cover, and simmer for 8 to 10 minutes. Do not puree; chunks of tomato should be visible.

DRESSINGS AND MAYONNAISE
Oil and Vinegar Dressing

MAKES ABOUT 1 CUP

¾ cup olive oil
¼ cup white wine vinegar
1 teaspoon sugar
salt
freshly ground pepper

1 Mix all ingredients until thoroughly blended.

2 Use immediately or set in refrigerator for later use.

Mayonnaise, by Hand and in Processor

MAKES ABOUT 1 CUP

½ cup olive oil
½ cup peanut oil
2 egg yolks
1 tablespoon Dijon mustard
1½ tablespoons fresh lemon juice
salt
freshly ground pepper

1 If making mayonnaise by hand, combine oils in a 1- or 2-cup spouted measuring cup and set aside.

2 Combine yolks and mustard in a heatproof bowl and whisk until combined. Put bowl over a pan with simmering water (bowl should not touch water) and whisk to a count of 10 or 12. The point is to warm the yolks; be sure not to cook them.

3 Remove bowl from heat and add oil about 1 teaspoon at a time, whisking constantly. As soon as each addition is incorporated, add more oil and continue until only ¼ cup oil is left. Whisk in lemon juice; when well incorporated, add the remaining oil. Season with salt and pepper to taste.

4 Mayonnaise can be thinned, if you wish, by adding a teaspoon to a tablespoon of warm water.

1 If making mayonnaise in food processor, combine oils in a 1- or 2-cup spouted measuring cup and set aside.

2 Combine yolks, mustard, and lemon juice in processor and blend for 2 or 3 seconds. With machine running, pour oil through spout in droplets, watching to be sure sauce is amalgamating. Continue pouring oil very slowly until all is used. Stop motor and season with salt and pepper to taste. Thin, if you wish, by adding a teaspoon to a tablespoon of warm water and processing 1 or 2 seconds.

Spinach Mayonnaise Collée

MAKES ABOUT 1½ CUPS

1 egg	1 cup fresh spinach leaf slivers,
1 teaspoon Dijon mustard	washed and dried
2 tablespoons fresh lemon juice	3 tablespoons chicken stock or
salt	vegetable broth
freshly ground pepper	1½ teaspoons white wine vinegar
½ cup corn oil	1 tablespoon dry vermouth
½ cup olive oil	1 teaspoon unflavored gelatin

1 Combine egg, mustard, lemon juice, salt, and pepper in processor and blend for 2 or 3 seconds. Mix the oils and pour in a very thin stream through feed tube, stopping machine when all oil is absorbed. Add the spinach and process for 4 or 5 seconds. Set aside.

2 In the top of a double boiler combine stock or broth, vinegar, and vermouth. Sprinkle gelatin over and let stand for 4 to 5 minutes or until gelatin is softened. Heat over hot water, stirring frequently, until gelatin is dissolved and mixture is clear and smooth. Remove from hot water and let mixture cool but do not let it thicken.

3 Transfer gelatin mixture to processor with mayonnaise and blend for 2 or 3 seconds. Turn into serving bowl and refrigerate until ready to use.

Mayonnaise Sour Cream Dressing

MAKES ABOUT ¾ CUP

¼ cup olive oil
1 tablespoon white wine vinegar
1 teaspoon sugar
¼ cup mayonnaise

¼ cup sour cream
salt
freshly ground pepper
light cream (optional)

1 Combine all ingredients except cream and blend until smooth.

2 If thinner sauce is desired, thin with light cream.

Basil Cream Sauce

MAKES ABOUT 1 CUP

1½ cups whipping cream
2 tablespoons finely chopped fresh
   basil or 2 teaspoons dried
salt
freshly ground pepper

1 In a saucepan combine all ingredients and bring to boil. Lower heat and simmer for 10 minutes, stirring often.

2 Strain through several layers of cheesecloth or a very fine strainer. Serve immediately.

Horseradish Cream Sauce

MAKES ABOUT 1 CUP

½ cup whipping cream, whipped
2 tablespoons grated horseradish
2 tablespoons mayonnaise
1 teaspoon dry mustard
2 tablespoons fresh lemon juice
½ teaspoon chopped fresh mint or
* generous pinch of dried*

1 Combine all ingredients by folding them into the whipped cream one at a time.

2 Continue to fold the mixture until well blended.

Tarragon Cream Sauce

MAKES ABOUT 1 CUP

1½ cups whipping cream
2 tablespoons chopped fresh tarragon
salt
freshly ground pepper

1 In a saucepan combine all ingredients and bring to boil. Lower heat and simmer 10 minutes, stirring often.

2 Strain through several layers of cheesecloth or a very fine strainer. Serve immediately.

Remoulade Sauce

MAKES ABOUT 1¾ CUPS

U se this sauce to accompany vegetables or to "butter" sandwich bread. Watermelon pickle provides a sweet-sour taste.

1½ cups mayonnaise
4 shallots, finely chopped
1 tablespoon anchovy paste
3 tablespoons chopped pickled
watermelon rind or sweet or dill
pickle
1 tablespoon chopped fresh tarragon or
½ teaspoon dried

1 tablespoon chopped capers
1 tablespoon Dijon mustard
2 tablespoons ketchup
2 tablespoons fresh lemon juice
1 teaspoon sugar
1 to 2 tablespoons whipping cream

1 Blend all ingredients except cream and refrigerate for several hours. To thin sauce, add heavy cream by the tablespoon to achieve desired consistency.

2 Mix again. Taste and adjust seasoning.

Sour Cream Dressing

MAKES ABOUT 1 CUP

1 cup sour cream
2 tablespoons sugar
2 teaspoons Dijon mustard
1 tablespoon white wine vinegar
salt
freshly ground pepper

1 Combine all ingredients in a bowl and whisk until smooth.

2 Taste and adjust seasoning.

DOUGHS AND BATTERS

Basic Pastry for Tarts and Quiches

This amount of pastry is enough for two 9- or 10-inch pie plates or two 10- or 11-inch tart or quiche pans, with enough for decorative cutouts in either case. If you make only one tart, prepare this amount of pastry anyway and freeze half of it; it keeps well in the freezer for several months. If you're just making 9-inch pie shells, there will be enough for three of them if you roll them out thinly enough and avoid any waste.

> 1 cup (2 sticks) chilled butter
> 6 tablespoons chilled shortening
> ⅔ cup ice water
> 4 cups sifted all-purpose flour
> 1 teaspoon salt
> 1 teaspoon sugar
> 1 egg white, lightly beaten

1 Cut sticks of butter in halves and then again in thirds lengthwise. Cut each length into ¼- to ½-inch cubes. Do the same with the shortening. Refrigerate both while measuring other ingredients.

2 Combine water and ice cubes in a 2-cup measure; when ready to use ice water, pour off all but ⅔ cup.

3 In an electric mixer bowl fitted with flat paddle beater (or by hand if you don't have mixer) combine flour, salt, and sugar. Add several pieces of butter at a time, keep the mixer going at medium speed, and keep adding butter bits until all is worked in. Continue with shortening. When mixture resembles small peas, add ⅔ cup ice water and mix only for a few seconds until dough forms into a ball, if some of the dough will not adhere, add 1 or 2 drops of ice water to dry bits of dough to complete ball. Remove from bowl and knead dough with palm of your hand for just a few seconds. Flatten ball into disk, sprinkle lightly with flour, and cut into 2 or 3 pieces. Wrap each in waxed paper and refrigerate for 30 minutes to 1 hour.

4 Remove dough from refrigerator one piece at a time. Roll out dough to fit pie or tart pan and cut out leaves or whatever for decoration. Lightly butter pan and fit in dough. Trim or crimp edge as you wish and refrigerate for 15 minutes. Prick the pie shell in several places. Cover pastry with foil or parchment paper, fill with rice, dried beans, or pie weights, and bake in preheated 425°F oven for 6 to 8 minutes. Remove weights and foil or paper and bake another 6 to 8 minutes or until pastry begins to brown. Remove from oven and set on wire rack. Brush with egg white while shell is still hot. Let cool before filling.

Crepes

MAKES ABOUT 12

3 eggs
1 cup water
1 cup all-purpose flour, sifted
½ teaspoon salt
melted unsalted butter for pan

1 For crepes, break eggs into a bowl and beat with a whisk. Add water and flour and whisk until smooth. Stir in salt and let the batter stand for 30 minutes.

2 Heat a 7-inch crepe pan or small nonstick skillet over moderate heat. Brush lightly with melted butter. Add about 3 tablespoons of batter and very quickly tilt and rotate pan until the batter covers the bottom (crepes should be thin, but substantial enough to handle). Cook until light golden on one side, then lift the crepe with a small thin knife or your fingers, turn, and cook the other side briefly. Slide the crepe out of the pan onto waxed paper. Repeat until all the batter is used, stacking cooked crepes between sheets of waxed paper. Brush the skillet lightly with butter after every third crepe.

15

KITCHEN NOTES AND COOKING TIPS

Here are some suggestions about certain foods and cooking techniques that we hope will be useful to you. These ideas are intended to improve the taste of food, clarify or simplify a cooking procedure, help you market for ingredients, or perhaps ease the strain on your pocketbook. It is not a glossary and that's why we call it "Kitchen Notes and Cooking Tips."

BAIN MARIE Many of our recipes call for a *bain marie* procedure, which is nothing more than cooking a dish of food in a pan which is set into another that has been half-filled with hot water. Think of a double boiler and you'll have the idea. Many of our preparations (loaves, timbales, etc.) are fairly delicate and require steady, gentle cooking. *Bain maries* are used in ovens and on stove tops. Actually, the water in a *bain marie* should not boil. It should simmer. In this way, the gentle steady cooking method is achieved. You don't need special equipment for this — just improvise by using a roasting pan, large casserole, or any oven-proof or heatproof vessel not too much larger than the container it will hold.

BLANCHING Blanching means boiling rapidly in lots of water for only a short time, for 1 or 2 seconds, for example. Vegetables are blanched for a variety of reasons: to set color, to aid in peeling, to destroy harmful enzymes, and at times to remove strong flavors (as in blanching orange and lemon peels).

PEELING ALMONDS Bring water to boil, add almonds, and boil just for a count of 5. Drain and remove skins by pressing each almond between your thumb and index finger while still warm. The skins will slip off easily.

BLANCHING BACON Before using it in a recipe it is usually advisable to blanch bacon by covering it with cold water, bringing the water to a boil, and boiling for 5 minutes. Drain and rinse the bacon under cool water, then dry it well and use as directed in recipe. This process reduces the salty, smoky bacon taste that can easily overpower other ingredients in the dish.

MAKING BREADCRUMBS We prefer drying out

bread in an oven and then crumbling it. The bread should be sliced, put in a 250°F oven and dried for about 30 minutes. It is then easy to grind the slices to crumbs in a food processor, but don't overprocess to powder. You can also run a rolling pin over the dried slices (carefully, as it has a way of scattering crumbs all over the work space). If you wish, sift the crumbs through a colander or strainer for uniform texture.

Boiling EGGS Properly hard-cooked eggs should not have a green outer yolk. We learned to boil eggs from Simone Beck; here are her suggestions:
a) rub a cut lemon over eggshell to keep it from cracking
b) don't use too large a saucepan; the pan should hold eggs in *one* large layer
c) place eggs in pan with *warm* water to cover and bring to a boil. From that point, time as follows:
  small eggs — 10 minutes
  medium eggs — 12 minutes
  large eggs — 12 minutes
d) put eggs immediately into cold water. Two minutes later, tap each egg against sink or bowl to break shell and let water seep between shell and egg. Shells can be removed easily in 30 minutes.

Skimming FAT Calorie conscious as we all are, it is always advisable to remove fat when making stocks, stews, and some soups. The easiest procedure is to chill the mixture until the fat congeals. It is then easy to remove, since it rises to the top. This can take overnight, though. If you need to degrease a stock quickly, line a strainer with several layers of cheesecloth and add some ice. Pour stock through into a bowl; fat will congeal as you pour (this is not as easy as just spooning fat from the top, but you can get most of it this way). After you've removed most of the fat, lay a paper towel on surface of stock to pick up additional droplets. Repeat with another paper towel if necessary.

PUREEING FOODS   We think a food mill is indispensable, and use ours all the time. It doesn't overprocess foods the way a blender or food processor can, and it removes tomato seeds and other unwanted vegetable parts such as strings and skins. Food mills come in various grades. Buy a good one, which won't tarnish and which comes with varying disk sizes. It's one of the cheapest and best kitchen utensils.

PEELING TOMATOES   Bring water to a boil and immerse tomatoes two at a time. Count to 10, then transfer tomatoes to a bowl of very cold water with a slotted spoon. To peel, cut out core first, turn tomato over, and cut away peel from bottom. With knife edge, peel and pull away skin. To seed, cut blanched, cored tomatoes in half and squeeze gently to remove seeds. If you want them seeded *and* pureed, put tomatoes through a food mill.

USING ZEST OF LEMON AND ORANGE   The zest is the colored part of the rind, with almost no pith (the white, bitter layer under the skin). Special zest peelers are available, and work well, but you can easily use an ordinary vegetable peeler without cutting deeply into the pith. We use the zest as fresh as can be — that is, as soon as it is peeled away and minced, we use it in the recipe. But dried zest works well, too, as its flavor lasts a long time.

BUTTER   Salted butter lasts longer than unsalted or sweet butter, but it is not as flavorful. We generally prefer the un-salted. To clarify butter, melt more than you will need of regular butter. When it is melted, spoon off the white foam which rises to the top. Pour off the yellow liquid after defoaming, leaving behind the whitish bits left at the bottom of the pan. The yellow liquid you pour off is the clarified butter, and it will keep in the refrigerator for several weeks at least.

CREAM Light cream is essentially the same as half and half, and neither will whip. Unless you need to whip it, you can use light cream in place of whipping cream to reduce calories. Sour cream can also be lightened by mixing in some yogurt. If we call for *crème fraîche* and if you can't find it, you can make your own by putting 2 tablespoons of sour cream or buttermilk into 1 cup whipping cream in a covered jar. Shake well and leave out overnight (or for most of the day) until the cream becomes thick; the time this takes will vary widely depending on room temperature. It will last for 5 or 6 days in the refrigerator. If you find real *crème fraîche*, it will be expensive — 4 or 5 times the price of whipping cream — but it is delicious.

FLOUR Most of our recipes call for all-purpose flour; unbleached is preferable to bleached. Instant flour is fine for certain uses but is not necessary, particularly in view of its added cost. Stone-ground flours are excellent, but remember that they won't keep as well as regular all-purpose. For prolonged storage keep stone-ground and other whole-grain flours refrigerated.

NUTS We use enough nuts to buy them in bulk and freeze them. We put frozen nuts straight into a food processor and have no trouble grinding or pulverizing them. If you are unfamiliar with pine nuts, try them. These are the kernels of certain pine cones and are especially delicious and flavorful when lightly toasted. Our recipes call for almonds, hazelnuts (or filberts), pecans, and walnuts. Walnuts and pecans are never blanched, but almonds and hazelnuts almost always are. Pine nuts come cleaned and ready to use.

OIL   We suggest the use of olive oil not because it is European but because it has more taste than other oils. Buy a good quality. Where we ask for olive oil, you may combine it half and half with peanut oil if you wish. Corn, vegetable, safflower, and sunflower oils are all abundant and good, but they have much less flavor than olive and peanut oils. Use them if you have reason to, or if called for in the recipe.

SALT   Kosher salt has no additives, and that is the reason we prefer it for cooking (and on the table, too).

VINEGARS   We like to use wine, cider, herb, Sherry, and fruit vinegars. There is a wonderful aged Sherry vinegar from Jerez, Spain, and another one of our favorites is beautiful raspberry vinegar. The Italian balsamic is delicious, but use very little of it in salads as it has a strong flavor. Basil, tarragon, and many other herbed and spiced vinegars have lots of uses in salads and elsewhere.

CONVERSION TABLES

The following are conversion tables and other information applicable to those converting the recipes in this book for use in other English-speaking countries. The cup and spoon measures given in this book are U.S. Customary (cup = 236 mL; 1 tablespoon = 15 mL). Use these tables when working with British Imperial or Metric kitchen utensils.

LIQUID MEASURES

The Imperial pint is larger than the U.S. pint; therefore note the following when measuring the liquid ingredients.

U.S.

1 cup = 8 fluid ounces
½ cup = 4 fluid ounces
1 tablespoon = ¾ fluid ounce

IMPERIAL

1 cup = 10 fluid ounces
½ cup = 5 fluid ounces
1 tablespoon = 1 fluid ounce

U.S. MEASURE	METRIC*	IMPERIAL*
1 quart (4 cups)	950 mL	1½ pints + 4 tablespoons
1 pint (2 cups)	450 mL	¾ pint
1 cup	236 mL	¼ pint + 6 tablespoons
1 tablespoon	15 mL	1+ tablespoon
1 teaspoon	5 mL	1 teaspoon

* Note that exact quantities are not always given. Differences are more crucial when dealing with larger quantities. For teaspoon and tablespoon measures, simply use scant or generous quantities; or for more accurate conversions, rely upon metric.

SOLID MEASURES

Outside the U.S., cooks measure more items by weight. Here are approximate equivalents for basic items in this book.*

	U.S. CUSTOMARY	METRIC	IMPERIAL
Apples (peeled and chopped)	2 cups	225 g	8 ounces
Beans (dried, raw)	1 cup	225 g	8 ounces
Butter	1 cup	225 g	8 ounces
	½ cup	115 g	4 ounces
	¼ cup	60 g	2 ounces
	1 tablespoon	15 g	½ ounce
Cheese (grated)	1 cup	115 g	4 ounces
Chocolate chips	½ cup	85 g	3 ounces
Coconut (shredded)	½ cup	60 g	2 ounces
Fruit (chopped)	1 cup	225 g	8 ounces
Herbs (chopped)	¼ cup	7 g	¼ ounce
Meats/Chicken (chopped, cooked)	1 cup	175 g	6 ounces
Mushrooms (chopped)	1 cup	70 g	2½ ounces
Nut Meats (chopped)	1 cup	115 g	4 ounces
Pasta (dried, raw)	1 cup	225 g	8 ounces
Peas (shelled)	1 cup	225 g	8 ounces
Potatoes (mashed)	2 cups	450 g	1 pound
Raisins (and other dried fruits)	1 cup	175 g	6 ounces
Rice (uncooked)	1 cup	225 g	8 ounces
(cooked)	3 cups	225 g	8 ounces
Spinach (cooked)	½ cup	285 g	10 ounces
Vegetables, (chopped, raw: onions, celery)	1 cup	115 g	4 ounces

* So as to avoid awkward measurements, some conversions are not exact.

DRY MEASURES

The following items are measured by weight outside of the U.S. These items are variable, especially the flour, depending on individual variety of flour and moisture. American cup measurements on following items are loosely packed; flour is measured directly from package (presifted).

	U.S. CUSTOMARY	METRIC	IMPERIAL
Flour (all-purpose	1 cup	150 g	5 ounces
or plain)	½ cup	70 g	2½ ounces
(bread or strong)	1 cup	125 g	4¼ ounces
(cake)			
Cornmeal	1 cup	175 g	6 ounces
Bran	1 cup	60 g	2 ounces
Wheat Germ	1 cup	85 g	3 ounces
Rolled Oats (raw)	1 cup	115 g	4 ounces
Sugar (granulated	1 cup	190 g	6½ ounces
or caster)	½ cup	85 g	3 ounces
	¼ cup	40 g	1¾ ounces
(confectioners	1 cup	80 g	2⅔ ounces
or icing)	½ cup	40 g	1⅓ ounces
	¼ cup	20 g	¾ ounce
(soft brown)	1 cup	160 g	5⅓ ounces
	½ cup	80 g	2⅔ ounces
	¼ cup	40 g	1⅓ ounces

OVEN TEMPERATURES

Gas Mark	¼	2	4	6	8
Fahrenheit	225	300	350	400	450
Celsius	110	150	180	200	230

Index